WINNING YOUR WAR AGAINST Satan

by Theodore H. Epp
Founder
Back t[illegible]

Back to the Bible
Lincoln, Nebraska 68501

Formerly titled *How to Resist Satan*

271,000 printed to date—1986
(5-4341—5M—76)
ISBN 0-8474-1123-0

Printed in the United States of America

Foreword

The Gospels and the Book of the Acts indicate that satanic activity was prevalent during our Lord's earthly ministry and the days of the early church. At no time since has that activity ceased entirely. Indeed, in all ages the child of God has been opposed by evil spiritual forces. But this glorious fact is also true: No believer has ever had to face the Enemy alone.

In his letters to Timothy, Paul predicted that, in the last days, seducing spirits would increase their activities and that the harmful effects of their false teachings would be felt everywhere. Other passages bear testimony to this same fact. As the Lord's return grows nearer, the fulfillment of these prophecies will stand out with increasing clarity.

Winning Your War Against Satan is a book for these times. It presents a well-rounded biblical discussion of the subject of Satan and the forces at his command. At the same time, it shows how Christians are "more than conquerors through him that loved us" (Rom. 8:37). This book describes how the Christian can lay hold of this victory and make it a part of his everyday experience.

Mr. Epp does not simply give us some armchair theories; instead he gives us some practical instructions based on God's Word and tested in the daily conflicts with the evil spirits around us. Because of God's great provision for us in Christ, believers can be victorious in every encounter with the forces of evil!

—The Publishers

Contents

Chapter 1

The Spiritual Warfare of the Christian

The reaction among Christians to the subject of spiritual warfare is varied. Some feel that it is a gloomy topic, not in keeping with the joy that should characterize the Christian life. Others take a seemingly morbid pleasure in such a subject, becoming filled with self-pity as they dwell on the heavy burdens they feel they have to bear. Neither attitude promotes spiritual health. It is equally vain to deny that such a warfare exists or, knowing that it does exist, to ignore it. All such wrong reactions please Satan and thwart the purposes of God in and through us.

In my early years of ministry, I knew very little about this subject. Some people came to me for help, but I had none to give. At the time I counseled with them, I sincerely believed I was helping them. But then suddenly I woke up to the fact that we Christians are in the midst of a spiritual warfare and that I knew little or nothing about it.

In spite of their discontentment and murmurings, the Children of Israel accomplished many things in the desert that pleased God. Forty years of discipline were needed, however, before the nation was ready to enter Canaan and engage in the type of warfare required to conquer the land. This truth awakened me to the fact that the Lord could not use me to the fullest unless I entered the spiritual warfare against the forces of evil intelligently and wholeheartedly. This, by the grace of God, I am now seeking to do.

Having missed this truth at the beginning of my ministry, however, does not mean that those early years were wasted. I was engaged in that warfare, whether I realized it or not. God does not wait until His servants understand all the details of the Christian life before He uses them. As our spiritual horizons are enlarged and our spiritual knowledge is increased, we become more useful to Him as we step out in obedience and faith to do His bidding.

The Reality of the Warfare

In any study about Satan, it is necessary that we first recognize the reality of the warfare that is currently in progress. The Book of Ephesians, felt by many to contain the highest truth regarding the Church, devotes a great deal of attention to the warfare we are considering. After dealing with various phases of the Christian's life on earth, the inspired apostle concluded with these words: "Finally, my brethren, be strong in the Lord, and in the power of his might. Put on the whole armour of God, that ye may be able to stand against the wiles of the devil. For we wrestle not against flesh and blood, but against principalities, against powers, against the rulers of the darkness of this world, against spiritual wickedness in high places" (Eph. 6:10-12).

The Twentieth Century translation of verse 12 is also helpful in understanding this struggle: "For ours is no struggle against enemies of flesh and blood, but against all the various Powers of Evil that hold sway in the Darkness around us, against the Spirits of Wickedness on high." These and other verses show us that we are involved in a very real, and very fierce, battle against Satan and his army. The only way we can win such a fight is by relying on the power of God and by preparing ourselves for the battle, using His instruments of warfare.

The Spiritual Aspect of the Warfare

As Christians, we have a tendency to overlook the spiritual aspect of our warfare. Too often we fight our battles strictly on the carnal plane—person against person or organization against organization. While we may have good reason to disagree with a man and his methods, it is not our business to fight the man. Instead, our responsibility is to fight the Devil, who has caused that man to leave the paths of righteousness.

At the heart of every struggle we face lie the powers of evil, who control the spiritual darkness around us. These foes, under Satan's direction, are exceedingly numerous and highly organized. But, as we have already noted, this should not cause us to become depressed. We need to know the character, power and methods of the Enemy in order to fight this battle intelligently. However, we must also remember that we are fighting a *defeated* foe. Remarkable as it may seem, our victory does not lie in having our minds occupied with the Enemy but rather in looking to Jesus, the Author and the Finisher of our faith (see Heb. 12:2). This gives us an enthusiasm in the fight and enables us to be "more than conquerors through him that loved us" (Rom. 8:37).

As this age draws to a close and the Second Coming of our Lord draws nearer, I am sure we will see greater opposition on the part of Satan to the Body of Christ. We must always keep in mind that the main battle is between Christ, the Son of God, and the Devil. The moment you and I accepted the Lord, we became members of the Body of Christ as surely as my finger is a member of my body. For this reason, we are continually under attack by Satan, for the venom of his hatred is aimed at Christ through us. But just as he lost his battle with Christ, so will Satan lose his fight with us when we learn to stand our ground against him in the grace and strength provided by our Saviour.

God Is Sovereign in His Universe

When we are in the midst of that real and violent spiritual struggle, we have a tendency to forget one vital fact: *God alone is all-powerful.* After the Lord had humbled Nebuchadnezzar, the Babylonian king honored God, saying, "And all the inhabitants of the earth are reputed as nothing: and he doeth according to his will in the army of heaven, and among the inhabitants of the earth: and none can stay his hand, or say unto him, What doest thou?" (Dan. 4:35).

Like man, Satan is a created being, dependent on the Creator for his life and power. He can do nothing without God's sanction. In describing God, the Scriptures tell us, "Who worketh all things after the counsel of his own will" (Eph. 1:11).

The Book of Job gives us a clear picture of God's ultimate and absolute sovereignty over His creation. While Satan was granted power over the elements and over men, at the same time the record shows that he could do nothing to Job without the Lord's permission. Furthermore, in afflicting Job, Satan could not go beyond the limits set by God.

The Bible tells us that this world's system is currently being controlled by Satan. The satanic forces are described as the "rulers of the darkness of this world" (Eph. 6:12), but they do *not* rule the universe. Without the preserving power of God, Satan could not operate for one moment. Nehemiah 9:6 tells us, "Thou, even thou, art Lord alone; thou hast made heaven, the heaven of heavens, with all their host, the earth, and all things that are therein, the seas, and all that is therein, and thou preservest them all; and the host of heaven worshippeth thee."

Satan overcame man in the Garden of Eden and has wielded a pernicious rule on the earth ever since. But, even in this capacity, Satan is a usurper who is tolerated by God for a limited time only. Each day brings Satan's judgment that much nearer.

Soon he will be chained and cast into the bottomless pit. At the end of the 1000-year reign of Christ, Satan will again be released for a short time, then taken and cast into the lake of fire, the place especially prepared for him and his angels (see Rev. 20:1-10; Matt. 25:41).

Satan's Limited Powers

In light of God's sovereignty and absolute control, we can see that while Satan is powerful, he is not omnipotent. He is clever, but he is not all-wise. Unlike God, the Devil is not present everywhere at the same time. Like any other created being, Satan can be in only one place at a time. However, he does have a vast company of evil spirits under his direction, and through them he knows a great deal of what goes on in the world. Though his influence is worldwide, nevertheless, he is subject to God.

But this influence in the realm of our spiritual warfare is not limited to the evil forces under Satan's control. God also has a heavenly host of His angels, who are ministering spirits to the heirs of salvation. This great army is fighting a constant battle against Satan's forces on our behalf. The psalmist tells us that "the angel of the Lord encampeth round about them that fear him, and delivereth them" (Ps. 34:7). This is not poetic imagination but a glorious fact.

This fact can be seen in the story of Elisha (see II Kings 6:11-17). Ben-hadad, the king of Syria, had sent an army to Dothan to capture this servant of God. This huge army arrived at Dothan during the night. When Elisha's servant went out very early in the morning, he was both startled and terrified to see the enemy surrounding the city. He rushed with the news to Elisha, who told him not to fear and then prayed, "Lord, I pray thee, open his eyes, that he may see" (v. 17). The Lord answered his prayer and opened the servant's eyes so that he saw a vast host of angels, with horses and chariots of fire, surrounding Elisha. The angels of God were guarding the prophet. This biblical account is one of those rare glimpses into the unseen that God has allowed us. It was written so that we might not despair when faced with the fact that we have powerful enemies.

We also find several references in the New Testament regarding the protection of angels. When Peter impetuously used his sword against a servant of the high priest in the Garden of Gethsemane, the Lord Jesus warned him to put it away. "Thinkest thou," said the Saviour, "that I cannot now pray to my Father, and he shall presently give me more than twelve legions of angels?" (Matt. 26:53).

Although God has not seen fit to give us extensive information regarding the part angels play in the affairs of men under His direction, enough is given to encourage us. The Bible presents us with a balanced view of the spiritual forces engaged in this spiritual warfare.

Although we are assured of victory in our spiritual battles, we should not regard this matter lightly. We are told that we must be sober and vigilant because our "adversary the devil, as a roaring lion, walketh about, seeking whom he may devour"

(I Pet. 5:8). The word "sober" refers to the sanity of our minds and indicates that we have no reason for becoming overly excited by Satan's attacks. Our Saviour told us that we should always pray, not growing fainthearted but trusting Him to deliver us (see Luke 18:1-8). Thus, practicing vigilance and keeping our minds under Christ's control are more than half the battle.

We are involved in an aggressive—not a passive—warfare. We cannot assume that because we have Christ as our Saviour and thus will ultimately be victorious, we can afford to ignore Satan. While it is true that he is not able to devour every person he hates, he can trip us up and cause our ministry for the Lord to be hindered. Therefore, it is vital that we know and understand our Enemy, especially his territory and his methods, so we can resist him. In order to remain steadfast in the faith, we must have a close walk with God and a constant, strong adherence to His Word.

Chapter 2

Satan Identified

The greatest battles Christ fought were against Satan, both in His own temptations (see Matt. 4:1-11) and on behalf of the people He was seeking to help (see Mark 1:23-27; 5:1-15). Likewise, Christians will face many tough battles with the Devil as he seeks to destroy the Spirit's influence in us. Our Enemy is not a mythical character but a person with great evil powers. Therefore, it is important that we learn everything we can about this foe in order to defeat him.

The New Testament makes it plain that this Enemy does exist. We read in Mark 3:22: "And the scribes which came down from Jerusalem said, He hath Beelzebub, and by the prince of the devils [demons] casteth he out devils [demons]." These men were fully aware of the fact that many evil beings known as "devils," or "demons," really existed. They also recognized that the demon forces were organized by the Prince of demons, known to them as Beelzebub.

The Lord Jesus, of course, rebuked these evil men for assuming that He was employing satanic powers to cast out evil spirits, but He did endorse the fact that such evil beings existed. He replied, "How can Satan cast out Satan? And if a kingdom be divided against itself, that kingdom cannot stand. . . . And if Satan rise up against himself, and be divided, he cannot stand, but hath an end" (vv. 23,24,26). Thus, our Saviour acknowledged that Satan is a person and that he has a kingdom under his control.

We find this same truth in the Book of the Revelation: "And there was war in heaven: Michael and his angels fought against the dragon; and the dragon fought and his angels, and prevailed not; neither was their place found any more in heaven. And the great dragon was cast out, that old serpent, called the Devil, and Satan, which deceiveth the whole world: he was cast out into the earth, and his angels were cast out with him" (12:7-9). Here again the Scriptures declare that Satan is a real being who is the leader of the evil angels.

My father was a missionary among the Hopi Indians in the early years of his ministry. He told us many hair-raising, but true, stories of his experiences with demons. He related how demons would come into the homes of the Indians and how the people would resist their presence. I do not know if the Indians could see the demons, but they could sense their presence and sought to drive them out by lighting small candles. When the Indians found that the candles did not wield any power against the evil spirits, they would run for the missionary. Again and again they bore testimony to the fact that when the missionary entered their homes, the demons went out another way.

Many liberal churches today have a tendency to treat Satan merely as an influence or as the concept of evil. They do not teach that he is a real person. But Satan is no mere influence or abstraction; he is a living personality. The Scriptures give an abundance of evidence to support this fact.

Proofs of Satan's Personality

In the Bible the pronoun "it" is never used in reference to Satan. Instead, the more personal words "he," "him," "thee" and "thou" are always used when speaking to him or about him (see Job 1:8; Matt. 4:10; John 8:44). Satan is never described merely as an influence either. When the Lord speaks to the Devil, He does so as He would to any person. In addition, the Scriptures attribute many deeds to Satan that could only be done by a living person (see Job 1:9-12; Matt. 4:1-11; I John 3:8; Jude 1:9). He walks about and influences people to sin. He instigates evil plans against God's people.

In I Peter 5:8 Satan is compared to a roaring lion who captures and devours anyone he can. An influence cannot roar or walk, but the Devil performs these functions. We further learn that he will be chained in the bottomless pit and finally will be placed in hell (see Rev. 20:1-3,10). You cannot bind an influence by a chain, but you can bind a person.

While Satan does not have flesh and blood as men have, for he is a spirit being, undoubtedly he can take on a visible form at will. However, we need to remember that flesh and blood do not make someone a person. The body merely provides the house in which the real person (man's soul and spirit) resides. When the body is laid in the grave, the person still lives on.

The Bible speaks of Satan about 175 times. In each case pronouns and names are given to him and deeds are attributed to him—all signifying that he is a person with great powers. While we have proof that Satan is a real person with real powers, we need to remember that "greater is he that is in you, than he that is in the world" (I John 4:4).

Names of Satan

The fact that Satan is not an influence but a person is also indicated by the names given to him. He is known in the Bible by a number of different names. The name "Satan" (see I Chron. 21:1; I Tim. 1:20) means "adversary" (see I Pet. 5:8)—a very appropriate name for the person who is the adversary of both God and man. His other common name, "Devil," is found in the New Testament but not the Old (see Matt. 13:39; John 13:2; James 4:7). As such, the Evil One is the slanderer and "accuser of our brethren" (Rev. 12:10).

In addition to these names, we find many other references to Satan that are significant and indicate his power, his work or his character. He is known as the "dragon," the meaning of which seems to be "serpent" or "sea monster" (see Rev. 12:3,4,7,9; 13:2,4; 20:2). Some other names are the Serpent

(Gen. 3:1; Rev. 12:9; 20:2); Beelzebub (Matt. 10:25; Mark 3:22; Luke 11:15,18,19); Lucifer (Isa. 14:12); the Wicked One (Matt. 13:19,38; Eph. 6:16); the Tempter (Matt. 4:3; I Thess. 3:5); the god of this world (II Cor. 4:4); the prince of the power of the air (Eph. 2:2); and the prince of this world (John 12:31).

We read in Revelation 12:9 that Satan is so great he can deceive nations. There is no question of the sinister power behind Communist-ruled nations and many other governments today. Satan is the master deceiver, and leaders of governments, in particular, are targets for his attack.

In the Gospel of Matthew we learn that Satan exerts power over the whole world. This, of course, speaks of the inhabitants of the earth who are not born again. In describing Satan's influence, Jesus said, "The field is the world; the good seed are the children of the kingdom; but the tares are the children of the wicked one; the enemy that sowed them is the devil" (13:38,39). Thus, this passage tells us that certain members of the human race are known as children in the Devil's family.

Hebrews 2:14 tells us that Satan once had the power of death. This power was wrested from him through Christ's resurrection, but the Lord still allows Satan to have a certain amount of power over death for the present. Even though everyone will die once, those who stand in the power of Jesus and hide behind His precious blood will not be touched by the second death. Thus, Satan's power over death is only temporary, for we will eventually be raised to live eternally with God.

The Origin and Career of Satan

A number of passages in God's Word tell us of Satan's origin and career. In Ezekiel 28:12 we read: "Son of man, take up a lamentation upon the king of Tyrus, and say unto him, Thus saith the Lord God; Thou sealest up the sum, full of wisdom, and perfect in beauty." In this verse it is especially important to note that while the king of Tyre is being addressed, the description seems to be directed at someone standing back of him—a being with greater force and power than any man could ever possess. This is no man but an angelic being who was created long before man was created.

It is not unusual for the Scriptures to use the name of an earthly country or high office to designate an angelic power. Take, for example, Daniel's experience recorded in Daniel 10. This servant of God prayed for 21 days in great agony of soul as he looked for an answer from God. Suddenly, at the end of those three weeks, an angel of the Lord appeared to him and said, "Fear not, Daniel: for from the first day that thou didst set thine heart to understand and to chasten thyself before thy God, thy words were heard, and I am come for thy words. But the prince of the kingdom of Persia withstood me one and twenty days" (vv. 12,13). Who was the prince of the kingdom of Persia? The rest of the passage sheds some light on his identity: "But, lo, Michael, one of the chief princes, came to help me; and I remained there with the kings of Persia" (v. 13).

Here we see that an angelic messenger sent from God was intercepted by an evil being called the "prince of Persia." This being could be none other than an evil angel who was Satan's representative over the kingdom of Persia. Michael, the archangel, came to the aid of God's messenger, enabling him to relay the word of the Lord to Daniel. Thus, in this passage we see that a human title was given to someone who was obviously an evil angel sent by Satan.

Going back to Ezekiel 28, we learn that the person addressed is "full of wisdom, and perfect in beauty. Thou hast been in Eden the garden of God" (vv. 12,13). Since the Garden of Eden was in existence long before the kingdom of Tyre, we can assume that the person spoken of here was not an earthly king but Satan, the serpent, who has been present since before creation (see Gen. 3:1-5,13-15).

In Ezekiel 28 a description follows the preceding verses that apparently refers to an Eden that existed prior to the one Adam dwelt in. In that original Eden, Satan was covered with every kind of precious stone (see v. 13). In verse 14 we read: "Thou art the anointed cherub that covereth." This could only refer to Satan, or Lucifer, in his original condition. The passage further states, "I have set thee so: thou wast upon the holy mountain of God; thou hast walked up and down in the midst of the stones of fire" (v. 14).

This picture of beauty soon changes to one of sin: "Thou wast perfect in thy ways from the day that thou wast created, till iniquity was found in thee"

(v. 15). These words could not be describing an earthly king, since none have been perfect.

The picture is darkened further as we read: "By the multitude of thy merchandise they have filled the midst of thee with violence, and thou hast sinned: therefore I will cast thee as profane out of the mountain of God" (v. 16). The events surrounding Satan's expulsion are given in Revelation 12:7-12. Because of Lucifer's sin, he was cast out of heaven, along with his angels, to roam the earth (see v. 9).

But this arrangement will not be permanent, for God will eventually judge and punish Satan for his sin (see v. 12). The prophecy in Ezekiel describes this judgment and punishment: "And I will destroy thee, O covering cherub, from the midst of the stones of fire. Thine heart was lifted up because of thy beauty, thou hast corrupted thy wisdom by reason of thy brightness: I will cast thee to the ground, I will lay thee before kings, that they may behold thee. Thou hast defiled thy sanctuaries by the multitude of thine iniquities, by the iniquity of thy traffick; therefore will I bring forth the fire from the midst of thee, it shall devour thee, and I will bring thee to ashes upon the earth in the sight of all them that behold thee" (28:16-18).

In Isaiah 14 we find the same subject, though other details are given that are not found in Ezekiel. We read: "How art thou fallen from heaven, O Lucifer, son of the morning! how art thou cut down to the ground, which didst weaken the nations! For thou hast said in thine heart, I will ascend into heaven, I will exalt my throne above the stars of God: I will sit also upon the mount of the congregation, in the sides of the north: I will ascend above the heights of the clouds; I will be like the most High. Yet thou shalt be brought down to hell, to the sides of the pit" (vv. 12-15).

Satan was once an angel of light, created by God to fill the responsibilities of the covering cherub—an angel who apparently protected the very holiness of God. Evidently he was the most powerful creature the Lord created and was second only to God in strength. But he was not satisfied with this position and desired to be like God. In fact, he tried to usurp the place of God and sit on His throne. Satan has not given up that hopeless pursuit even yet.

In contrast to Satan's origin, the Lord Jesus was not created but was present in the beginning with God (see John 1:1,2). He had no beginning Himself but created everything else in the universe, including the angel Lucifer (see v. 3). Satan, on the other hand, is not eternal in the sense that God is. When creation's work was begun by the Lord Jesus, Satan was not there. He was created as an angel of light and possibly served for millions of years in that position before he fell. Like all created beings, the Devil had a beginning; however, he will have no end, as he is doomed to spend eternity in hell.

We see the character of Satan in the fact that he knew the truth but did not abide in it. He allowed his pride to control him; and since pride goes before destruction, we find that wherever Satan goes, trouble and destruction follow. Those who choose to follow him are doomed to be just like him. John 8:44 tells us, "Ye are of your father the devil, and the lusts of your father ye will do. He was a murderer from the beginning, and abode not in the truth, because there is no truth in him. When he speaketh a lie, he speaketh of his own: for he is a liar, and the father of it."

Satan has been a murderer and a liar from the time he sinned against God. The very depth and breadth and height of sin are his, for his nature is evil, and darkness is his abiding place. Furthermore, he is not alone; he has a great company of evil spirits with him. His kingdom is thoroughly organized, and he works through his evil forces, seeking to impose his program on men and governments. We are continually in combat with Satan and the lesser powers under him. He freely roams the earth, spreading his evil in every corner.

But as we struggle against the Devil, we can be encouraged by the knowledge that he will not be free forever. Revelation 20:10 tells us, "And the devil that deceived them was cast into the lake of fire and brimstone, where the beast and the false prophet are, and shall be tormented day and night for ever and ever." God will eventually bring Satan's evil course to an end and will confine him in hell for eternity.

Chapter 3

Satan's Kingdom

The Scriptures, as well as human experience, teach us that many of the mental and spiritual conflicts a Christian faces as he serves the Lord are due to the opposition of spirit beings. Countless numbers of demons belong to the kingdom of Satan and act under his direction. They try to discourage, distress, perplex and harass those who are seeking to honor Christ with their lives.

In the first two chapters we have learned that we are surrounded by a kingdom of darkness comprised of various ranks of evil spirits, with Satan as their head. Since they cannot reach the Lord Jesus Christ, they have turned the focal point of their attack against believers—Christ's representatives in this world. Christians are part of His Body; therefore, the satanic forces seek to destroy the Body by opposing its service and spiritual growth.

In order to fight the forces who are trying to destroy us, we need to understand Satan's kingdom so we can recognize his work when we see it. According to Ephesians 6, Satan's kingdom is comprised of four major divisions: *principalities, powers, rulers of the darkness* and *wicked spirits in heavenly places.* We read in verse 12: "For we wrestle not against flesh and blood, but against principalities, against powers, against the rulers of the darkness of this world, against spiritual wickedness in high places."

At the head of these different divisions is Satan himself. Under him are demon forces and fallen angels. Some may wonder about this, but the fact that certain angels fell with Satan is clearly stated in the Bible. In Matthew 25:41 we read that hell has been prepared for the Devil and his angels. Further proof of the existence of evil angels is found in Jude 1:6, where we learn that there are certain angels who, at the present time, are reserved in chains. They will be included in that great future judgment when Satan and his evil followers will be thrown into the lake of fire.

Principalities

The first of these divisions in Satan's kingdom is called the *principalities.* In several places the Bible alludes to the fact that Satan has divided this world into sections, or provinces, that are each controlled by a prince (demon). The word "principalities" has special reference to political realms in which evil spirits work to influence earthly rulers, kings, presidents, parliaments, legislatures, judges, civil officers, voters, party politics, office holders, office seekers and the entire range of men and matters connected with the government.

The prince of Persia spoken of in Daniel 10 is one of these principalities. Daniel had prayed concerning his people, but he had to wait 21 days before the answer finally reached him. A powerful evil angel, known as the "prince of Persia," had hindered the message. It wasn't until Michael, the archangel, came to the rescue of God's first messenger that this evil being was overcome and the message was finally delivered to Daniel (see vv. 1-14). This incident is illuminating in several respects. First, it proves beyond the shadow of a doubt that evil angels do seek to influence world governments and, whenever possible, to hinder God's plans. It also shows that by persevering prayer, God's people can defeat the purposes of the Enemy.

Without a doubt, all earthly governments—from the national government on down to its smallest segments—are attacked by evil spirits. These demons seek to manipulate and influence people who are in office. Whether the government officials realize it or not, some of the pressure brought against them stems from the fact that Satan and his organized forces are trying to force these influential people in the direction they want them to go.

We sometimes find Christian men and women who have been providentially placed in office, but even they are not immune from attack by these principalities. This is one reason why such leaders have difficulty at times giving clear-cut answers on some issues. The antagonism they experience is not primarily from those who oppose them. The real source is Satan. No wonder we are instructed to pray for those in government! When we do, we resist and thwart the efforts of the Enemy in persuading men to follow the path he has mapped out for them.

Powers

The second division in Satan's kingdom is referred to as *powers*. The word represents an exceedingly large section of evil spirits in Satan's army who possess great energy and force. Their particular method of operation is to attack the personal feelings and thoughts of Christians. Unbelievers are also attacked in this way, and the terrible crimes we repeatedly read and hear about in the news are, without a doubt, in some way inspired by these evil powers. What method they use will depend on the individual and whether or not he is a Christian.

These demons do not show their real colors to us when they make their appearance. They operate behind the disguises of self-interest, self-gratification and revenge. These are powerful stimulants to evil action in themselves, but when encouraged by evil beings, they can result in the lowest and foulest kind of deeds. Those guilty of such actions may never even realize that evil spirits have added their persuasive powers to the base desires inherent in the human heart.

Some people may even justify their wicked and cruel actions by thinking they are doing it for God. This was true of Saul of Tarsus before he realized his awful sin against Christ and the people of God. It was not until he was saved that Saul saw how he had been the dupe of satanic forces.

As we have already noted, these powers attack a

person's feelings and thoughts. When a person is unprovoked, he is less likely to react violently when a false accusation or derogatory remark is made against him. While it is true that we all have an adamic nature that urges us to resent these injustices, human reactions are greatly intensified when the natural prodding of our fleshly nature is combined with outside stimulation by demons. I am sure that many church quarrels are initiated by these powers. This seems to be the only reasonable explanation for the hatred engendered in some of these arguments and for the fact that many such quarrels last for generations. Service for God under such conditions is almost impossible, and great shame is brought on the cause of our Lord.

Defaming a person's character is also one of the functions of these evil spirits. The powers of Satan work on our minds and tongues so it becomes much easier to say something evil about a person than something good. However, when we are under the direction of the Holy Spirit, this tendency is reversed and we are able to do and say what is good rather than what is destructive.

Every person has certain defense mechanisms built into his personality. When someone makes a comment that appears threatening to us, our first reaction is to rise to our defense. It is not unusual in a family to have someone ask a question and have the person respond in anger, "Well, I told you so a long time ago." Why does the person react this way? The reason is that he is seeking to justify himself against the charge of forgetting to pass along some information that should have been given earlier. Many times evil spirits are behind these comments, seeking to stir up unrest in families and among people in general.

Among the nefarious works performed by demons is that of raising up talebearers among the believers. While it is true that Satan is called the "accuser of our brethren" (Rev. 12:10), often he does this work by using Christians to accuse their fellow believers. Yet nine times out of ten, if those Christians who are at odds with each other would lay all the facts on the table regarding their disagreements, they would very likely find no real reason for having hard feelings toward each other. It is true that bad feelings should not exist among Christians at all, but the sad fact is that such feelings often exist when the people have no good reason for them, even from a purely human standpoint.

Christians need to face this matter squarely. Satan's powers are working in hearts and minds, seeking to destroy peace in the lives of God's people. This apparently is their particular assignment, and their hard work is leading to much success for Satan's kingdom.

Rulers of the Darkness

The third division in Satan's kingdom is known as the *rulers of the darkness* of the age. While the King James Version uses the word "world" in Ephesians 6:12, the Greek word here is more accurately rendered "age."

Who are the rulers of the darkness that we wrestle against today? They are evil spirits who foster superstition, fortune-telling and false teaching of various kinds. The work of these satanic forces is evident in many activities so prevalent today—astrology, witchcraft, the occult and the vast array of religious cults. These rulers of darkness are not new. Satan has been using them in his kingdom since the beginning of time, and the Bible warns us to beware of their practices (see Deut. 19:10-12).

Vast multitudes in this world, even in our so-called civilized nations, are highly superstitious. Even those who do not participate in the occult or astrology practice milder forms of superstition. Seeing a black cat will frighten some people, and many possess a horseshoe, rabbit's foot or some other "lucky" object. The rulers of darkness breed this kind of superstition, holding untold millions in spiritual slavery.

For the Christian, the most dangerous work the rulers of darkness perform is that of deluding people into watching for signs, seeking the interpretation of dreams or following mental suggestions and emotional impressions they receive—regardless of the source. Jesus warned us that false teachers would come who would perform signs, leading away even the elect (see Mark 13:22,23). Today we possess God's complete revelation to man in His Word. He speaks to us through the Bible, and the Spirit interprets the Word to our hearts. Therefore, Christians, of all people, should avoid any extraordinary means for trying to discover the will of God.

Wicked Spirits in Heavenly Places

The fourth group in Satan's kingdom is the *wicked spirits in heavenly places,* which is an accurate translation of the expression "spiritual wickedness in high places" (Eph. 6:12). These are religious demons who intrude into the highest religious experiences. They come as angels of light, sometimes speaking through men behind pulpits—giving these unregenerate men the false ideas that continually lead so many astray.

In some cases, these wicked spirits control the thinking in religious schools. This is certainly true where modernism and higher criticism have taken over. We also see their handiwork in the Jehovah's Witnesses and other religious cults, who do not even know the Greek language yet seek to change the meaning of many words in the Bible in order to substantiate their unbiblical teachings.

Some of these evil spirits will pose as the Holy Spirit Himself. Many of the so-called demonstrations of the Holy Spirit are actually manifestations of these evil spirits. Many earnest people have been drawn into such movements through ignorance and have been exposed to the worst types of demonism. I have had to deal with some individuals who have been deceived by these groups, and by the grace of God, I have witnessed their cleansing from the vexation of these demons and their happy release from these powers (see Acts 5:16).

This particular division of Satan's kingdom works primarily in religious circles—the "heavenly places." In Ephesians 2:2 Satan is described as the "prince of the power of the air." His presence is felt even in churches. These wicked spirits see to it that certain people join churches and yet are unsaved. These people are baptized and profess religion. They may even claim to possess holiness. They sometimes speak of having marvelous dreams, give prophecies and claim to have wonderful spiritual gifts, but they are not saved.

The purpose of the wicked spirits in heavenly places is to attack the most conscientious religious people and get them to accept heresy and to follow impressions until they become conceited and self-righteous, fancying themselves to be above others.

The Pharisees and scribes are good examples of people who were being influenced by these wicked spirits. Jesus said of them, "Ye are of your father the devil" (John 8:44). In his first letter the Apostle John wrote: "He that committeth [continues in] sin is of the devil" (I John 3:8). In that same letter he added, "We know that we are of God, and the whole world lieth in wickedness" (5:19). In this world man can only be in one of two places—in the hands of Christ or in the lap of Satan. Unfortunately, too many people, including some "Christians," have joined the forces in Satan's kingdom.

Satan's kingdom is vast, well organized and responsive to his bidding. He has millions of evil angels, demons and men on earth assisting him in a variety of areas. These spirits are seeking to control every government and leader on earth. They attack the thoughts and feelings of both Christians and unbelievers, inspiring all sorts of violence, quarrels and unrest. His forces are in control of many dark and foreboding superstitions and practices, and they are even infiltrating the teachings of the Church, leading many people astray. But while Satan's power and influence are great, our Saviour's power is greater still. Christ can help us overcome Satan's forces when we trust in Him.

Chapter 4

Satan's Methods

Satan uses a variety of methods in his attempt to control the lives of people. Most of these strategies are very deceptive, appearing to be perfectly harmless on the surface. However, in reality, his wiles are deadly, and Christians must enter the battle with their eyes wide open in order to successfully resist these temptations. Thus, it is vital that every believer understand the methods employed by Satan in order for their faith to remain strong.

The Bible gives us some very clear, and very strong, instructions concerning our attitude toward Satan. First Peter 5:8,9 admonishes us, "Be sober, be vigilant; because your adversary the devil, as a roaring lion, walketh about, seeking whom he may devour: whom resist stedfast in the faith." The Twentieth Century translation says, "Exercise self-control, be watchful. Your adversary, the Devil, like a roaring lion, is prowling about, eager to devour you. Stand firm against him, strong in your faith."

The type of watchfulness being described in these verses is not simply looking around to see if the Devil is near, for we will not see him. The way to watch is through the Word so that when he casts his darts and seeks to trap us in his wiles, we will be protected. Begin each day by reading God's Word and discovering what the Lord wants you to do—then walk with God throughout the day. In this way you will be applying the protection of His blood that will keep you safe from Satan's darts.

The Strategy of Satan

One of the Devil's greatest masterstrokes in his war against Christ and His people is his ability to hide his identity. Some years ago we had a visitor in our home—a man who walked with God. As he talked with us, he perceived in his soul that we needed help. We did—*spiritual help.*

The man told us that the Lord had sent him to pray for us. He asked if we had anything in particular that we needed prayer for. We replied that we felt as if we had some hidden needs that we could not quite identify but that were problem areas.

He said, "Let me tell you something. What we need to do is unite our hearts together in prayer and ask God to expose Satan."

In other words, Satan was doing some underhanded work and needed to be exposed, and only God could expose him. The Lord gave us wisdom in this matter and showed us what needed to be done. He also showed us how we could claim victory over the Evil One by applying His Word.

Satan likes to come as an angel of light. In this fashion he works very much like sugarcoated pills. The pill is bitter, but you do not know it because it tastes sweet and looks good. The coating makes it palatable. Likewise, Satan can make us believe that some of the things we are doing are for God when, in reality, they are deadly sins hiding under a facade of righteousness.

A good illustration of this comes from the Old Testament. In Joshua 9 we read of the deception of Joshua by the Gibeonites. The great battle of Jericho had just been won and Ai had been taken when the Gibeonites came. They knew from the Israelites' victories that soon the Gibeonite strongholds would be in the hands of the Israelites. So, wanting to preserve their own lives, these wily strategists put on old clothing, took dried-up bread with them and made it appear as if they had traveled a great distance. They completely deceived Joshua, who thought from the bread, the clothing and the shoes that the Gibeonites were a distant people who were genuine in their desire for a treaty with the Israelites. No doubt their request flattered Joshua, and so he did not ask the Lord what he should do. As far as we know, this is the only time that Satan caught Joshua off guard, but catch him he did. The Bible says of the Israelite leaders: "They asked not counsel at the mouth of the Lord" (v. 14). In other words, they were not watchful.

The league was made with the Gibeonites, and though their deceit was soon discovered, Joshua had to live up to the treaty he had made to preserve these people. The Gibeonites became servants to the Israelites and lived among them, becoming a constant source of trouble to the Israelites and leading them into pagan worship.

This is one of the methods Satan likes to employ against the Christian. If he can deceive us, he will. This is why we need to be watching constantly—daily surrendering our wills to the Lord and filling our minds and hearts with His Word and with the fruit of the Spirit. When we are doing these things, Satan will not be able to find a loophole in our defenses.

Another of Satan's wiles is to misquote Scripture or mislead people in the interpretation of Scripture. We are living in an age of great confusion, with new "isms" creeping into our civilization continually. Someone claims to have a vision, while another person takes a verse and uses it out of its context. These and many other methods are being used by false teachers in order to gather a following. There are many other ways in which Satan operates in this realm, but in every case his method is designed to keep people from the real truth found in God's Word.

Satan likes to keep people so busy with nonessential matters that they have no time for the essentials. For instance, social service is being emphasized in some churches today, while the Gospel of Christ's shed blood is being left out. The efforts on the part of these churches are merely humanitarian. In one sense these efforts are good, but yet they are also evil because of what they displace.

At one point in my life, I was struggling greatly with Satan because of my interpretation of Philippians 2:13: "For it is God which worketh in you both to will and to do of his good pleasure." Notice here the two aspects of God's work in us: He works in us both "to will" and "to do." For many years God burdened my heart to do His will. I sincerely wanted to do it, but I stumbled when it came to actually doing His will. I did not see the connection between this verse and other passages of Scripture. I thought that if God instilled in me the will to do His bidding and gave me the power to do it, all I had to do was to sit back and wait passively on Him. So even though I had the right desire, my lack of understanding about God's methods kept me from accomplishing anything for Him.

Such passivity is not God's way. His will is active. I was seeking to do God's work in the same way that I pick up a pencil and make it do my work. A pencil or a pen is simply a passive tool in my hands. They have no power or choice. But man is not made that way. God created man with a personal will and desires. He expects us to make our own choices and act on them after we have sought His will. Thus, Philippians 2:13 is saying to us, "I will perform my will in you. I will give you the desire, but you must follow through in the work according to My directions."

God opened the Jordan River to Joshua and the Children of Israel, but they had to march into the riverbed and across it. God did not carry them over. When I saw that truth, I could no longer sit idly by, twiddling my thumbs and saying, "Well, do it, Lord." When I made the first move, God continued to lead me and to open up the way, blessing His work as I stepped forth in obedience to Him. I had to learn that lesson the hard way.

Satan's strategies are many. His forces are continually at work around us. Satan often hides his identity and convinces us that what we are doing is the Lord's will when it isn't. He misquotes Scripture and misleads us in the interpretation of God's Word in order to confuse us and keep us from a proper understanding of the Bible. He seeks to keep us busy with nonessential activities so that we do not preach the Gospel as we should. And he deceives us into thinking that God will control us like a puppet so that we sit back and do nothing as we wait on the Lord to reveal His will to us. Therefore, we must always be alert and aware that the Enemy is lurking nearby so that he will not overcome us.

Satan's Methods With Religious People

The words "religion" and "Christianity" are not synonyms. Many religions in our world today (and not only the "heathen" ones) are not Christian in any sense of the word. Likewise, a good number of Protestant people have religion, but that does not mean they have Christianity.

One of Satan's most successful methods of deception is convincing people that being a "good, moral person" is the same as being a Christian. The Devil's best representative on earth is the person who has high morals and is apparently honest and kind but is still unsaved. Many people are led to believe that this kind of life-style will win them a place in heaven, even though they have no regard for God in their hearts. Satan lures more people into his net with this type of thinking than with any other means of deception. He is the promoter of all systems of religion, including those that teach good works or morality as a means of salvation. It is not necessary to go to non-Christian nations to find these systems. They are everywhere.

The Children of Israel were very religious in Paul's day; however, they were living by works and not by faith. Paul said of them, "For they being ignorant of God's righteousness, and going about to establish their own righteousness, have not submitted themselves unto the righteousness of God. For Christ is the end of the law for righteousness to every one that believeth" (Rom. 10:3,4). What was said of Israel could be said of many persons today, persons who are ignoring the righteousness of God that comes by faith and are seeking to substitute their own righteousness for that of Christ's.

One of the ways Satan convinces people that their own righteousness is sufficient to save them is by playing down the awfulness of sin and the fact that man is a sinner and needs to become a new creature in Christ Jesus. Many churches have given in to this type of thinking and are leaving the blood of Christ out of their message to the world. They present Jesus merely as a martyr or a great teacher. The Devil is pleased with this kind of preaching, for it omits man's need to be saved by accepting Jesus as Saviour. Christ's death on the cross meant Satan's defeat, for His death and resurrection provided salvation and eternal life for all. Thus, Satan fears the Gospel message more than anything and seeks to silence it.

In place of Christ's message of regeneration, Satan is preaching one of reformation and self-development. When we hear such a message, we must remember that Satan's emissaries are presenting it. These people may be very sincere and utterly blind to what they are doing, but Satan is not. Nothing pleases the Deceiver more than bringing unbelievers into the pulpits of our country to spread a message that leaves out the finished work of Christ. These men may speak knowledgeably and brilliantly on many subjects. They may speak persuasively of the fatherhood of God and the brotherhood of man; but whether they know it or not, they are speaking on behalf of the Evil One and not God.

The theme of Satan's kingdom is man-made righteousness. However, the Bible teaches us that no person is righteous (see Rom. 3:10,23). The only way to achieve the righteousness of God is by accepting Christ as Saviour and having His shed blood applied to us personally (see vv. 21-26). Only those who are born again will see the kingdom of God.

In addition to convincing people that having good morals and being involved in many "religious" enterprises is enough to be saved, Satan seeks to keep Christians from witnessing concerning Christ. One of the ways Satan hinders some Christians in their witness is by causing them to think that dealing with the lost is for preachers only. In fact, many congregations today feel that they "hire" the preacher for just that purpose. Remember, however, God has told us in His Word that every person is to witness for Him wherever he is (see Matt. 28:19,20; Acts 1:8).

Besides deceiving some into not witnessing at all, Satan causes still others to preach another "gospel." Many false teachers today use the name of our Saviour without knowing anything of His real purpose in coming into this world. Many of them teach a "social gospel" that emphasizes how the world can be made better through the humanitarian works of church people. Those who preach this type of message place an emphasis on education, legislation, better standards of living and so on. Many of these things are not wrong in themselves, but when God's people are expected to concentrate all their efforts toward these ends, to the exclusion of telling others about Christ, then it is wrong.

Paul enunciated the great purpose of the Gospel when he said that he did certain things so that he "might by all means save some" (I Cor. 9:22). He knew that he could not save every person or even civilization as a whole. He did not even try. However, the apostle knew he could tell men and women of Christ and reach some of them with that glorious message. Paul realized the fact that a social order is no better than the individuals in it. Only as individuals are transformed by the power of Christ can their environment be changed for the better.

In I Timothy 4:1,2 we are warned that in the last

days doctrines of demons will prevail. A form of godliness will exist, but the essential power will be denied. We are currently living in that age, and its terrible results can be seen on every side.

Many religious leaders today practice the worst form of deception—they use the same phrases as Christians but attach entirely different meanings to them. Thus, many people, including some Christians, are being deceived by their outward show of godliness. But, in reality, these false teachers are denying the basic doctrines of Scripture—the sinfulness of man and redemption through Jesus Christ, the Son of God.

We need to remember that Satan fell, not because he aspired to be a fiend but because he wanted to be equal with God. He has implanted that same purpose and plan in the hearts of men and women today. They are aspiring to be like God without a new life in Christ Jesus. But their efforts will only end in failure for themselves and for all who listen to them. Evidences of this spiritual breakdown are multiplying daily in our world.

Satan's Wiles With the Christian

In the Scriptures Christians are frequently warned against the wiles of the Devil. Our Saviour spoke about these snares to His disciples on several occasions. Paul and Peter sounded strong warnings in their epistles concerning the Evil One and his subtle traps. In each case the warning is given to the saved—not the unsaved. Ephesians 6:11 instructs

God's children, not unbelievers, to put on the whole armor of God so they can be strong in the Lord.

However, many Christians have the mistaken idea that as long as they know God they can ignore the Enemy and still win the battle. This delusion is one of Satan's cleverest devices. Much of the Deceiver's success lies in the fact that he so cleverly hides his identity that people do not suspect his evil presence or his purposes. Using these tactics, Satan and his evil forces seek to gain control of the believer and to dominate his life. Therefore, it is vital for believers to know the methods Satan employs to both oppress and obsess whomever he can among God's people.

Satanic Oppression

The Apostle Peter, in speaking to the household of Cornelius concerning Jesus, said, "God anointed Jesus of Nazareth with the Holy Ghost and with power: who went about doing good, and healing all that were oppressed of the devil" (Acts 10:38). The word "oppress" is significant. It means "to exercise control over" or "to tyrannize." The indication is clear that such oppression is not from within but from without and comes from satanic forces.

One of the methods the demons use in oppressing the saints is that of placing them under great mental and emotional pressure. You hear much about this condition today, but I assure you that a Christian does not have to live under such pressure. He can be free from it even though it is all around him. We can overcome these pressures when we put on the whole armor of God and remain strong "in the power of His might" (Eph. 6:10).

A striking passage with regard to the battle for control of the believer's mind is II Corinthians 10:3-5, where we read: "For though we walk in the flesh, we do not war after the flesh: (for the weapons of our warfare are not carnal, but mighty through God to the pulling down of strong holds;) casting down imaginations, and every high thing that exalteth itself against the knowledge of God, and bringing into captivity every thought to the obedience of Christ."

From this passage it is clear that our war with Satan is not a physical but a mental one. Satan, through his evil forces, is constantly attacking the hearts and minds of believers in order to put them under pressure. These pressures may come at work, at home or at church. Often Christians do not even recognize the real source of their trouble—Satan—and may blame other people or situations for their problems. Thus, we need to identify Satan as the source of these strains and seek to bring our thoughts in captivity "to the obedience of Christ" (v. 5) so we are not overcome by oppressive thoughts and emotions.

A number of years ago I received a letter from a missionary that illustrates this point very well. His communication showed that he was having victory over satanic forces on the mission field. For example, when he lost his passport, he stated, "It could have gotten me very vexed, for what Satan wanted was to spoil the image of Christ in me. He wasn't concerned about my passport. I acknowledged that it was Satan, and I took the victory stand against him; and then I found my passport." He named three or four other incidents that had happened to him in which he was able to discern that Satan was trying to oppress him. With regard to them he said, "I found the victory in Christ every time, and then the other things were straightened out too."

We need to remember that the Devil is already a defeated foe (see Heb. 2:14; Col. 2:15). Thus, we can be victorious over Satan's oppressions when we oppose him directly in Jesus' name and claim the power of Christ's blood as our protection.

For a number of years I felt these pressures. At times, in order to find relief, I got into my car and drove out into the country to have a talk with God, and eventually the depression left me. Then one day I realized that such pressure could be coming from Satan. I knew the way of victory in the Word and took it. Since that time it has not been necessary for me to take my trips to the country to relieve this heart and mind pressure, because I found the way of victory. God gave me discernment to see that satanic forces were causing this depression in an effort to control me.

Satanic Obsession

After Satan has scored success in oppressing the Christian, he takes up the second phase of his work—*obsession.* Many times in the New Testament we see Jesus and the apostles healing a variety of illnesses, including demon obsession.

Luke 6:18 tells us, "And they that were vexed with unclean spirits . . . were healed." Note especially the word "vexed" in this passage. We find this word again in Acts 5:16: "There came also a multitude . . . bringing sick folks, and them which were vexed with unclean spirits." The word "vex" comes from a Greek word meaning "to obsess," "to harass," "to mob" or "to riot." It speaks of a vicious attack made by demons upon a person.

We see a prime example of satanic possession of an unbeliever in Matthew 12:43-45. A demon had been driven out of a person. Once the evil spirit left, he was forced to wander around looking for another home. Finding none, he returned to the one whom he had originally controlled and found that the person was not filled by the Holy Spirit but was merely reformed (empty). Then the demon called in seven others to help him harass this person. They came like a flood and began to attack his mind.

While an unsaved person is being described in this passage, we know from other passages that satanic forces will also attack the minds of Christians from without, even though they cannot gain control of their spirits. They suggest doubts to us, especially doubts concerning the goodness of God. Instead of having the mind of Christ, we suddenly begin to dwell on the thoughts suggested by one of the demons. A mind obsessed by Satan thinks evil of God. In order to avoid this, we are told, "Let this mind be in you, which was also in Christ Jesus" (Phil. 2:5).

As we have already noted, the mental powers of a

believer may be affected by demons. In II Corinthians 10:3-5 we see that not only the unsaved but the saved as well can have their minds obsessed by evil ideas about God. We need the Lord's powerful weapons for the "pulling down of strong holds; casting down imaginations, and every high thing that exalteth itself against the knowledge of God" (vv. 4,5). This passage is not describing a few depressing thoughts but an all-out mental war against God led by the evil forces controlling our minds.

Let's look at some of the ways these demon powers try to harass Christians in order to cause evil thoughts about God. Possibly the most common method they use is *worry*. Instead of having the peace of God that would keep our emotions in proper balance and our minds thinking correctly, we worry needlessly about our problems. Prolonged anxiety can even cause us to blame God for our situation, ultimately leading some to reject Him.

While worry is a natural emotion, Satan seeks to capitalize on this anxiety and use it to take control of the believer's mind. But God can give us His peace that will expel our worries if we will only ask Him. I thank God that He has helped me so that if I have any worries, I am not aware of them. Rather than feeling anxious, I am enveloped in a sense of God's peace and love. This is the best protection against Satan's fiery darts of worry.

In addition to worry, Satan also uses *discontentment* to gain control of our minds. Rather than fretting about our situation and feeling dissatisfied with it, we need to follow the example of Paul, who said, "I have learned, in whatsoever state I am, therewith to be content" (Phil. 4:11). When we learn to apply this important principle to our lives, then no problem that Satan may place before us will cause us to stumble into the pit of discontentment.

A third way Satan harasses Christians is by causing them to have a *complaining spirit.* Many people succumb to the temptation to always see the dark side of life. Of course, some believers have a greater problem with this than others, but Satan fosters this type of attitude in the hearts of almost everyone in order to gain control of their minds.

"Oh, it's my nature" is the explanation that Christians often give when confronted with this truth. I agree that the tendency to complain is part of human nature but would also add that it is Satan working through their nature. Do not at any time excuse yourself for some weakness on the basis of your nature. When Jesus Christ died, the old nature was crucified with Him (see Rom. 6:6). Each day we must continue to nail the desires of that old nature on the cross. The Lord can help us to do this and also to live by the new nature that He has given us.

Vain imagination is another of Satan's tools. He can cause us to imagine all kinds of wild thoughts, even believing that someone hates us. I talked to an unsaved woman not too long ago who imagined that everyone hated her, including God. Satan was certainly obsessing her mind. Even Christians may feel this way. When we find ourselves struggling with unrealistic thoughts, we can dispel them by reading the truths in God's Word and by asking the Lord to give us a clear mind. When we prayerfully consider these thoughts, we will soon realize just how foolish they really were.

In addition, Satan places evil thoughts about others in the minds of God's people. He often does this by tempting us to attribute wrong motives to their actions. This type of thinking is another form of vain imagination.

Along with evil thoughts about others, we often struggle with *impure thoughts*, which seem to run rampant at times. I remember one incident where this problem was very apparent. A man I knew came to our door at 1:00 a.m. one night. As he stood there, I saw that his eyes were staring and his face was white with fear.

I invited him in. After a brief pause, he cried, "You've got to help me, Brother Epp! You've got to help me!"

He then began to pour out, in vile language, the most impure thoughts I have heard since I was saved. Immediately, I said to him, "Man, do you know what's happened to you? Satan has taken possession of your mind."

He answered, "I know it."

We then prayed for his healing. God gave the victory, and the man was released from this obsession. The stare left his eyes, and the color returned to his face. He got up and said, "Thank you, Brother Epp. That's all I needed."

Of course, this was an extreme case of Satan's

work in our thoughts. However, while many of you have not gone that far, no doubt Satan is vexing your mind with a number of impure thoughts. If you allow these thoughts to continue and to grow, you may be setting yourself up for satanic obsession of your mind.

We have touched on only a few of the means that Satan uses to harass and control our minds. In addition to worry, discontentment, complaining, vain imaginations and evil and impure thoughts, the Devil may also use anger, harshness, suspicion, fanaticism, irritableness, a critical spirit, a spirit of revenge, fear, grief, contention, impatience, sensitiveness, pride, frustration, heresy, conceit, jealousy and many other thoughts and emotions to obsess us. We must constantly be aware of these emotional temptations and allow God to control us so that we do not become obsessed by them.

Satanic Control

How far can Satan go in controlling a Christian? In order to answer this, we first need to consider what the Bible teaches about man. According to I Thessalonians 5:23, every person is composed of body, soul and spirit. Thus, man is a trinity.

By calling to mind the picture of the Old Testament temple, which contained the outer court, the Holy Place and the Holy of Holies, we can readily see the meaning of I Corinthians 3:16: "Know ye not that ye are the temple of God, and that the Spirit of God dwelleth in you?" The word for "temple" here refers to the innermost sanctuary, the Holy of

Holies. The New Testament also uses another word translated "temple" that refers to the entire temple. According to this verse, the Spirit of God takes up residence in the spirit of the Christian and stays there. This inner spirit can never be possessed by any demon because God will never leave it, for He has promised, "I will never leave thee, nor forsake thee" (Heb. 13:5). In an analogy of the Jewish temple and the Christian, we can see that the spirit of the Christian corresponds to the Holy of Holies, the soul (mind, emotions and will) to the Holy Place and the body to the outer court of the temple.

Taking this analogy one step further, we need to remember that the inner sanctuary did not need to be invaded before the temple, as such, was defiled. The Jews were guilty of defiling their temple on more than one occasion. At the time of our Lord's public ministry, the Jews were selling cattle and doves for sacrifice in the outer court of the temple. Jesus drove them out, saying, "Make not my Father's house an house of merchandise" (John 2:16). Thus, we see that they had defiled the whole house by defiling part of it.

This fact reveals to us the importance of having every part of our lives fully surrendered to God. No wonder we read in Romans 12:1: "I beseech you therefore, brethren, by the mercies of God, that ye present your bodies a living sacrifice, holy, acceptable unto God, which is your reasonable service." This sacrifice includes not only our spirits but also our bodies and minds: "Glorify God in your body, and in your spirit, which are God's" (I Cor. 6:20).

God wants complete possession of each of us—a possession that includes body, soul and spirit, for if one part is defiled, all is defiled.

Neither Satan nor any of his demons can possess anything that is controlled by Jesus Christ and the Holy Spirit. But the Evil One can control areas not indwelt by the Holy Spirit. As we have stated before, when a person is saved, the Holy Spirit takes up permanent residence in his spirit. Therefore, that part of the Christian can never be controlled by Satan. As far as the unsaved person is concerned, the Devil can possess all of him or her.

In the case of the Christian, if his soul and body are also surrendered fully to God, they are filled by the Spirit, and Satan can have no part of them. This is one reason why we are admonished to be filled with the Spirit. When we turn our entire being over to Him, Satan cannot touch us.

We have some concrete illustrations in the Scriptures of persons who were believers but did not surrender themselves fully to the control of the Holy Spirit. In I Corinthians 5 Paul cites the case of an immoral man who brought great shame to the cause of Christ. His body was being used by Satan for purposes of immorality (see v. 1). Paul told the other church members, "Deliver such an one unto Satan for the destruction of the flesh [the body], that the spirit may be saved in the day of the Lord Jesus" (v. 5).

The chastisement given to this man was severe, but it achieved its intended purpose. The man realized his sin and sought forgiveness before God and his fellow believers. Consequently, the Apostle Paul later instructed the believers to receive the man back into fellowship (see II Cor. 2:5-11).

The principle operative for such punishment is found in I Corinthians 3:17, where we read: "If any man defile the temple of God, him shall God destroy; for the temple of God is holy, which temple ye are." This passage describes man as the "temple of God." Just as defilement of the outer court of the Jewish temple defiled the Holy of Holies as well, a wrong use of the body (the outer court of man's temple) defiles the inner sanctuary (man's spirit).

God does not view this kind of defilement lightly. The words "defile" and "destroy" in this passage are the same word in the original Greek text. Thus, this verse could be translated, "If any man mar the temple of God, him shall God mar" or "If any man corrupts the temple of God, God shall bring him to corruption." Therefore, the word "destroy" is not referring to annihilation, as some people often interpret it, but a temporary, severe punishment for the purpose of cleansing.

Another illustration of satanic control in an area of a Christian's life is found in Acts 5. Ananias tried to lie to the apostles about his offering to the Lord, but Peter stopped him, saying, "Ananias, why hath Satan filled thine heart to lie to the Holy Ghost?" (v. 3). Because Ananias had not given the Holy Spirit control of all of his heart, Satan was able to work in him so that he became greedy and lied. Any Christian who is not filled with the Holy Spirit is open territory for the work of demon powers.

There was a time in Peter's own life when he let Satan take control momentarily and he uttered words that were rebuked by Jesus. The Lord had just foretold His death and resurrection. Peter rebuked Him for His words, saying, "Be it far from thee, Lord: this shall not be unto thee" (Matt. 16:22). It is apparent that Peter did not realize the gravity of what he had said. He was actually seeking to set aside the entire redemptive program that God had established long before the fall of man.

The Saviour turned to Peter and said, "Get thee behind me, Satan: thou art an offence unto me: for thou savourest not the things that be of God, but those that be of men" (v. 23). Jesus realized that Satan had possessed Peter's mind for an instant and had spoken through him. You will notice that the Lord Jesus did not say in His rebuke, "Get thee behind me, Peter" but rather "Get thee behind me, Satan." Satan was speaking through Peter, causing him to utter words that were at variance with the revealed will of God.

It is likely that Peter learned a lesson from this experience that he never forgot and that he never again allowed Satan to control him to such a degree.

In his letter to the Ephesians, Paul urged, "Neither give place to the devil" (Eph. 4:27). This verse admonishes us not to give Satan any space in us where he can work. We all have certain areas in our lives that could be turned over to him, whether we are conscious of them or not, so we must guard ourselves continually to prevent Satan from gaining a foothold in our hearts.

Thank God it is not possible for Satan or any of his demons to take complete control of a Christian, since he has the Holy Spirit within him. But we must avoid giving any room to the Devil, for he will take what ground is not surrendered to the Spirit of God if he can. Satan will oppress us and will seek to break down our resistance in order to gain control of certain areas of our being; however, the way of victory is simple and is available to us at any time. Satan's strategies and methods will have no effect on us when we are completely filled with the Holy Spirit and are allowing Him to control us.

Chapter 5

Satan Is a Defeated Foe

In speaking about the Church, the Lord Jesus stated that the gates of hell would not prevail against it (see Matt. 16:18). This passage assures us that, as members of the Body of Christ, we will ultimately be victorious in our fight against Satan. Christ won the war with Satan through His death and resurrection; thus, we are fighting a defeated foe. While Satan may win a few skirmishes now and then, he will lose in the end.

Throughout the Bible we find God's promises of victory over Satan and his army. The first such promise was given after the fall of man (see Gen. 3:15). In this verse God stated that the seed of the woman (Jesus Christ) would someday trample the head of the serpent (Satan). In ancient times it was the custom for a conqueror to demonstrate his victory over a foe by placing his foot on the neck of the defeated enemy. This act indicated that the enemy had been completely subdued. In our battle with the Devil, we need to remember that Satan's head is resting firmly under the foot of Christ. The Enemy has been completely subdued; therefore, we have nothing to fear, even though he may roar like a lion against us.

The cat and the dog are a good illustration of how the Christian should react toward Satan. Ordinarily, if a cat has a safe place to run to, it will do so. However, when no tree or safe spot is within reach, the cat will turn around, arch its back and spit at the dog. When this happens, the average dog will turn and walk away from the fighting cat. We, too, must be like a cat and call Satan's bluff. When we face the Devil squarely and resist his advances, he will turn tail and run (see James 4:7).

Philippians 2:8-11 also describes the victory we have over Satan through Jesus Christ. After describing how Christ humbled Himself and was obedient, even to death on the cross, we learn that God highly exalted Him. He gave Him a name above every name "that at the name of Jesus every knee should bow, of things in heaven, and things in earth, and things under the earth" (v. 10). Every living creature in heaven, on earth and *in hell* is subject to Jesus Christ; therefore, the Lord is in control of Satan. Anything that the Devil can do is simply being allowed by Christ for the present.

The Basis of Victory

The basis of our victory lies in the fact that Satan was defeated by Christ at the cross. There He judged the Devil and overthrew him (see John 12:31,32; 16:11). Because of our Saviour's great work on the cross, believers have overcome Satan: "And they overcame him by [on account of] the blood of the Lamb, and by [on account of] the word of their testimony" (Rev. 12:11). The blood here refers to Christ's death. Not only are we saved from sin on account of that death, but we are also saved from Satan.

This brings to mind our union with Christ. We must be identified with Him in His death. When our old nature is crucified and buried with Christ, then we are also raised to a new life on earth and eternal life in heaven with Him (see Rom. 6:4-9; Gal. 2:20). What happened when Jesus Christ was crucified, buried and rose again? He was taken from the earthly kingdom into the heavenly kingdom, where no one on earth, not even Satan, could touch Him.

Since we are identified with Christ in His death, we are no longer affected by Satan's threat of death. This great truth is illustrated in the example of the Children of Israel in Egypt (see Ex. 12:1-13). God instructed the Israelites to sprinkle the blood of a lamb on the doorposts of their homes. When the death angel came at the appointed time to slay all the firstborn of Egypt, those who were in the homes with the blood on the doors were safe, for the death angel passed over them. He could do nothing because of the blood. So it is in the case of Satan. He cannot enter past the blood of Christ.

The blood of Jesus stands as a great wall between us and the Evil One. It covers our sins, cleanses our hearts and minds and protects us from his advances. Although we may not understand how this can be true from the human standpoint, we do not need to. All we have to do is believe what God says.

In our position before God, we have already died to sin in Christ. He has forgotten our sins entirely. However, in our daily walk we must also consider ourselves dead to sin, not allowing it to reign over us again (see Rom. 6:11-13).

Further light is given on this subject in Hebrews 2:14,15, where we read: "Forasmuch then as the children are partakers of flesh and blood, he also himself likewise took part of the same; that through death he might destroy him that had the power of death, that is, the devil; and deliver them who through fear of death were all their lifetime subject to bondage." Colossians 2:15 adds, "And having spoiled principalities and powers, he made a shew of them openly, triumphing over them in it [His death on the cross]." The Greek word in Hebrews 2:15 translated "destroyed" means "to render powerless," "to render useless," "to cancel," "to bring to an end." Thus, we see that Satan's power has been broken through Christ's death.

Our Saviour stripped Satan of his power so that he is actually powerless against the Christian who obeys the Lord in spiritual warfare. Without a doubt, Satan thought he was the conqueror when Christ died; but the real truth is that Satan was overcome by virtue of that death. Because of Christ's death, believers can also defy all the powers of Satan and render them useless.

Referring again to Israel's experiences in going from Egypt to Canaan, we find in the death of Pharaoh a clear picture of the truth under investigation here. God miraculously opened the waters of the Red Sea for the safe passage of the Israelites. This is a picture of death. The Egyptians followed hard after them but did not catch them. As soon as God's people had safely reached the other shore, Moses stretched his rod over the sea, and the waters returned, drowning Pharaoh and all his host. The sea that had been the means of Israel's deliverance became the means of Pharaoh's defeat. So it is with Calvary. Jesus died on that hill, but in dying He destroyed, or brought to an end, the power of Satan. Since that time Satan has been a defeated foe.

Since this is true, why then is Satan still active? He is a usurper and an outlaw, and he will not give up his attacks on us unless we stand on the victory gained by Christ at Calvary. We enjoy the fruits of that victory as we appropriate it by faith in our daily walk.

The Power for Victory

In speaking of the glorious power that we enjoy in Christ, Paul stated, "How fathomless the depths of God's resources, wisdom, and knowledge! How unsearchable His decisions, and how mysterious His methods! For who has ever understood the thoughts of the Lord, or has ever been His adviser? Or who has ever advanced God anything to have Him pay him back? For from Him everthing comes, through Him everything lives, and for Him everything exists" (Rom. 11:33-36, Williams). All wisdom, all power and all resources belong to God. He will use us in this great battle against Satan and will pour out His power to us to the extent that we let Him.

In Ephesians 6:10 we read: "Finally, my brethren, be strong in the Lord, and in the power of his might." Our strength is not a human strength; it is the strength of God made available to us through Christ. When this power is exercised, it spells defeat for Satan and his forces.

I have seen irrigating systems on farms in the area and have had the opportunity to examine some of the reservoirs used. Some of these reservoirs would be filled at night with pumps, and the water would then be used for irrigation during the day. Such were the limited resources on some of those farms.

However, the reservoir of power spoken of in Ephesians is as great as God Himself. God's power and man's power can be compared to an ocean and a single drop of water. On one hand we have God's power—larger than the ocean itself—and on the other hand we have man's power—a mere drop of water in a bucket. In Ephesians God reveals to us something of this mighty power available to us. The knowledge of this power does not come by human philosophy or reasoning; it is revealed. Paul, in praying for believers, said, "The eyes of your understanding being enlightened; that ye may know . . . what is the exceeding greatness of his power to us-ward who believe, according to the working of his mighty power, which he wrought in Christ, when he raised him from the dead, and set him at his own right hand in the heavenly places" (1:18-20).

We need to recognize who our foe is and how strong he is in comparison to us, but we must not magnify his strength beyond that of Christ's. Satan is a defeated foe. As Christians, we have more than enough power in Christ to overcome Satan. David went against Goliath in the name of the Lord, and though all David had was a stone and a slingshot, he had all that he needed. This Old Testament incident reminds us of the great work of Christ as stated in Colossians 2:15: "And having spoiled principalities and powers, he made a shew of them openly, triumphing over them in it." Satan met his defeat at Calvary.

The Source of Victory

Satan is a powerful foe. No human being can hope to cope with him without divine help. A believer cannot take the offensive against him, but he can resist him. The word "resist" means "to withstand the force or effect of" or "to exert oneself so as to counteract or defeat."

The word "resist" also indicates that we are not to flee from the Enemy. Courage is called for in this fight against Satan, courage that only God can give. Satan and his forces are forced to flee when the Christian stands his ground in the might of the Lord. This standing, or maintaining, of our ground is the goal in this battle (see Eph. 6:13).

The Book of Ephesians gives ample proof that God will give His child the needed strength for the conflict. In chapter 1 we read of the "exceeding greatness of his [the Father's] power to us-ward who believe" (v. 19). The armor that the Christian is to wear in the conflict points to Christ (see 6:11-17).

In this same passage the Holy Spirit's contribution in helping us fight the battle is emphatically expressed. It is through prayer, controlled and directed by the Holy Spirit, that we put on and keep on the armor of Christ and find ourselves empowered by the Father (see v. 18). Each member of the Trinity has a part in the believer's victory over the Evil One. We must always remember that our help lies in God and not in ourselves. Humble yourselves under God's hand, and He will exalt you (see I Pet. 5:6). With infinite power on our side, Satan and his army of demons cannot stand against us.

The Channel of Victory

Jesus Christ, God the Father and the Holy Spirit, then, are the source of our victory over Satan. In this present age they channel that power for victory through the members of the Body. Jesus Christ is the Head of the Church, and as members of His Body, we carry out His will. Christ plans the war strategy, but He uses us to accomplish the task.

It is for this reason we are told in Ephesians 6 to be strong in the Lord and in the power of His might (see v. 10). There is no other power by which we can overcome the Enemy. And just as our physical muscles increase in strength through use, so will our spiritual muscles become stronger as we consistently wage this warfare against Satan. We need to stand our ground against Satan and allow Christ to work through us.

It sometimes takes extreme cases to bring some of these matters to our attention. Several experiences in my own life have convinced me of the power of Christ that is channeled to those who are willing to be used.

A few years ago a couple came from another state to see me. According to what they told me, the wife had been a Bible teacher and a soul winner for years and had given herself wholly to the Lord's work.

However, when they came to see me, she had stopped winning souls. She was living under fear and dread. So great was her fear that when her husband went off to work, she would go over to the neighbors, for she could not bear to be alone.

Her disposition had changed. She was tormented with the thought that she had committed the unpardonable sin. Her witness for the Lord had been silenced.

I encouraged her to confide in me and tell me what had taken place in her life previous to that time of depression and uselessness. As she talked, I prayed that the Lord would open my eyes to see where the heart of this problem really lay. All at once I saw what was wrong. She thought she had opened her heart to the Lord for more spiritual power, which would have been good if it had been true. But instead of believing that God had accepted her commitment, she had waited to see what would happen. The Lord tells us to commit ourselves to Him and He will use us. For some reason, however, she had not believed this. She had ceased to trust in God. Faith was eclipsed by sight. She waited for something to happen, looking for an experience or a feeling of some sort. This gave Satan the opportunity he needed to deceive her. He first persuaded her to doubt and then to fear.

Fortunately, she was a woman with a good grasp of the Bible, and she accepted my analysis of the situation without difficulty. I advised her to take an open stand against the Evil One in the name of Jesus, believing that since He had conquered Satan, she would conquer as well. I encouraged her to openly and vocally resist Satan in the name of Christ. She followed my advice. Soon after that, they left my home, and I did not hear from them for several months. When they did contact me, I was overjoyed to receive the news that she was back in the service of the Lord again and had a refreshing testimony for Him. The demon of fear had been completely overcome, and she was cleansed.

It is true that this is an extreme case, but unfortunately, it is not an isolated one. Such attacks by Satan seem to be on the increase among God's people. In the majority of cases, the Devil usually is not able to win such complete victory. However, he often succeeds in hindering us in some way.

I remember dealing with a Christian brother some years ago who prayed that God would resist Satan. I immediately broke into his prayer and said, "Brother, that's not what God told you to pray. If you want release, you tell the Devil in the name of Christ that you are resisting him. Take your stand." The man then took his stand against Satan and was released. The spiritual tension in his life was suddenly lifted. That man learned this important lesson: *God does not fight our battles against Satan for us.* Instead, he uses us as channels through which His power can flow to resist and cast down the Enemy of our souls. That strength does not lie in us—it lies in Christ—but He accomplishes this victory through us.

However, in considering our role in resisting the Devil, we must be careful not to place undue emphasis on this subject, as some have done in the past. In fact, this past emphasis may be one of the reasons why so many present-day Christians fail to take this subject seriously. They draw back from it because of extreme positions held by some in the past. The fact remains, however, that the command to resist the Devil is from the same Lord who told us to be filled with the Holy Spirit. Sooner or later each Christian who is seeking to be filled with the Spirit will have to face situations in which he or she must resist the Devil. Many times in our lives we will face, and be forced to combat, the satanic forces that control the spiritual darkness of this world (see Eph. 6:12; II Cor. 11:14).

God has not left the job of resisting the Devil to a select few whom He has chosen for that task. His admonition to fight Satan has been given to every believer. Every person who is born into the family of God must live out his earthly life in a sphere where he is constantly challenged by the forces of Satan.

The Book of the Revelation confirms the fact that every believer is called to resist Satan. Christians are to overcome "by [on account of] the word of their testimony" (12:11). God wants His victory over the Devil enforced through us by means of our spoken testimony. We know that the Lord Jesus rebuked Satan directly (see Matt. 4:10). The archangel, Michael, also rebuked Satan in the name of the Lord (see Jude 1:9). The Apostle Paul directly addressed the evil spirits in the demon-possessed girl in Philippi and in the name of Jesus cast them out of her (see Acts 16:16-18). Apparently, the rebuking of evil powers in the name of Jesus was customary, for the sons of Sceva tried to imitate Paul in casting out a demon. However, because they lacked the personal application and benefits of the shed blood of Christ, they were soundly beaten by the demoniac (see 19:13-16).

Thus, we see a definite pattern in the Word for rebuking Satan verbally. While this is not always the case, it may often be necessary to rebuke Satan in the name of the Lord in order to keep our prayers and other areas of our Christian lives free from satanic hindrances.

At this point, some may be asking, "How can we address Satan personally and rebuke him in the name of the Lord?" You may say something similar to this when withstanding the Adversary: "I died with Christ; therefore, you have no more power over me. In the name of Jesus Christ, I rebuke you, Satan!"

Techniques for Victory

Besides channeling His power through the believer, God has also given us instructions for appropriating that power in our fight against Satan.

A key passage dealing with the techniques for victory is James 4:7: "Submit yourselves therefore to God. Resist the devil, and he will flee from you." The divine order for successful resistance is that we first submit to God and then we can resist Satan. Failure on our part to submit to God means defeat at the hands of the Enemy.

The language used in this verse is a picture of warfare. We are to "submit," as a good soldier places himself under his military leader. The word "resist" means to stand bravely against the foe. When we are submitting to God, our Commander in Chief, and are following His leadership, then we will have the courage to face the Enemy and the power to win the fight.

As believers, we should carefully evaluate every situation we face and every choice we must make. Our prayer should be: "If this is of God, I will accept it. If it is of Satan, I will resist it in Christ's name." Throughout the Gospels, we find the Saviour doing this very thing. When the Devil tempted Him to take the easy road to victory, Jesus saw that it was not from God and resisted Satan (see Matt. 4:1-11). In the Garden of Gethsemane, Jesus prayed that He might not have to experience the suffering of the cross, if it was God's will. However, He realized that it was His Father's will for Him to die, and He accepted it willingly (see 26:36-46).

We see this victory in Abraham's life when he offered his son, Isaac, without questioning God's command. When Abraham demonstrated his submission and obedience, God reiterated His promise to make him the father of a great nation (see Gen. 22:1-18).

We also see in this story that some time passed between God's command to Abraham to offer up his son and the moment when the Lord intervened and provided a ram in place of Isaac. Likewise, there are times in our experience when the Enemy is allowed to rage, but only until we demonstrate our full submission to God. The Lord wants to give us victory over Satan. If we seem to be missing that victory, it is probably due to our lack of submission to God.

We must learn to wait for God's timing in all things. However, too often we are like the sisters of Lazarus, who chided the Saviour for not coming soon enough to keep their brother from dying. Why did Jesus delay coming? It was not because of a lack of love for Lazarus and his sisters, for we read that Jesus wept at the grave of Lazarus (see John 11:35). He delayed in order that the submission of those involved might be complete and that the victory over death, the enemy, might be even greater. Proof of our submission lies in the testing. The quicker the submission, the sooner the victory.

The submission spoken of in James 4:7 is not a passive attitude but an immediate act of obedience to God and an aggressive resistance against Satan. A Christian who does not realize that he needs a greater degree of submission to God and more prompt obedience is on dangerous ground. In fact, the closer we walk with God, the more we realize how much we need new life from Him.

In seeking to surrender ourselves more fully to God, we must beware of the methods Satan often uses in tripping up God's children. Like the psalmist, many of us have said, "Search me, O God, and know my heart: try me, and know my thoughts: and see if there be any wicked way in me" (Ps. 139:23,24). This kind of examination is good as far as it goes, but we must not stop there. To throw open the door in such a manner without going any further gives Satan the opportunity he wants. He will dig up some old sin that God forgave long ago and will harass our conscience with it. When we begin to dwell on a past sin, we are forgetting a very practical truth the Apostle Paul stressed: "Forgetting those things which are behind" (Phil. 3:13). When sins are under the blood, we should not continue to dredge them up and dwell on them.

Dr. T. Myron Webb often used the following illustration in his discussion of this subject: Some individuals wanted to see what happened to a person when he died. So they buried a dead cat but left the tail sticking above the ground. Each day they would go out to where the cat was buried and pull it up again. Every day, of course, they saw the carcass of the cat become more decomposed. Soon the stench was sickening. Although they could hardly stand to be near the grave, they kept going back. Many Christians treat their old sin exactly the same. Even though it has been buried under the blood of Christ and forgiven, they continue digging it up.

When you ask the Lord to reveal any wickedness

in your life, you can be sure that He will show you some things that are wrong. As you discover these sins, immediately ask God's mercy for them and thank Him for putting your entire life under the blood. In this way you will not give Satan an opportunity for using these old sins as a stumbling block (see I John 1:9).

I know a man who was in a mental hospital for a time because of this very problem. When I was able to show him how to resist Satan and when he took a stand for Christ, he was delivered.

The same thing took place in the life of a missionary in Africa. For a long time she labored under a load of sin that Satan had dug up. She became ill from it. The mission board was ready to send her back home when God used some missionary friends to deal with her and show her that these sins had been forgiven. She finished her term on the field and was able to return to Africa after a furlough, where God used her for many more years.

In addition to submitting ourselves to God, the Lord also instructs us to be alert and calm in the face of battle. This technique will enable us to be victorious. First Peter 5:8,9 tells us, "Be sober, be vigilant; because your adversary the devil, as a roaring lion, walketh about, seeking whom he may devour: whom resist stedfast in the faith, knowing that the same afflictions are accomplished in your brethren that are in the world." The Williams translation of this passage uses the word "calm" in place of the word "sober." This tells us that we are to face the Devil in the name of Jesus Christ without any fears, trusting Him to enable us to resist Satan's wiles.

We are also admonished to be vigilant, or alert. This is not an alertness born of fear but is rather an acute awareness that comes through the study of the Word. Here we find not only warnings about Satan and his devices but also detailed instructions for how to resist him. Most importantly, the Bible encourages us with the fact that Satan has been defeated by Christ and is powerless against Him. As Christians, we have the unlimited power of Jesus Christ available to us through the Holy Spirit. When we submit ourselves to God and are obedient to Him in spiritual warfare, we can rebuke the Devil and he will flee from us. No matter what Satan may try to do to us, we can experience victory in the Lord.

Chapter 6

The Christian's Armor

Any experienced soldier knows that in order to win a battle and keep from being killed you must have effective weapons and proper protection. This is also true in our war with Satan. He is attacking us with every weapon he has. If we enter the battle against him unarmed and unprotected, we are in danger of being destroyed. However, God does not send us into the battle with Satan unprepared. In Ephesians 6 we find a description of the spiritual armor that the Christian has been given to protect him in this fierce combat with the Enemy and his armies (see vv. 13-17).

In order to enjoy full victory against the Devil, we must put on the whole armor of God (see v. 11). *The Amplified Bible* reads: "Put on God's whole armor—the armor of a heavy-armed soldier, which God supplies—that you may be able successfully to stand up against [all] the strategies and the deceits of the devil" (v. 11).

This armor is not to be put on periodically. We receive this armor when we become a Christian and are to put it on at that time and never remove it again. However, as we develop in our Christian life, we will continually readjust our armor as we discover weak spots in our lives that need to be covered. But this adjustment process will not require us to run back to God in order to have the armor put on again. The act of surrender described in Romans 12:1,2 is a once-for-all act. This is followed by an attitude of heart that maintains our act of surrender from day to day.

The purpose for putting on the whole armor of God is that we might be able to stand our ground when the evil day comes (see Eph. 6:13). To wait until that day arrives and we are facing a severe temptation would be too late. Neither is it enough merely to put on one or two pieces of the armor. All of it must be worn if it is going to be effective. Some of us succumb to Satan's attacks either because we have failed to put on the armor or because we have failed to wear all of it.

For example, most of us have a constant battle with our tempers. We may find ourselves under some kind of strain, caused perhaps by illness, economic distress or stressful situations at work or at home. Then something happens that triggers our resentment. Perhaps we are unjustly criticized or are simply not appreciated. This gives Satan an opportunity to fire one of his darts at us, and we succumb. The result is we lose our temper. If we would learn to walk with the Lord at all times and to keep our Christian armor where it belongs, we would find it much easier to deal with these feelings before they lead to a fit of anger.

By wearing the armor of God, we are able to

stand against Satan. But the Scriptures also warn us to beware of the counterattacks of Satan. Because we have defeated the Devil once in a given situation does not mean that he will give up. He is a tenacious foe and is not easily discouraged. But God assures us that the armor will not only give us victory the first time but will also protect us against the subtle and vigorous counterattacks of our Enemy.

We must always remember that Satan is a defeated foe. He may roar like a lion, but we do not need to fear the noise he makes. When we stand firm in the victory we have received in Christ, Satan is the one who must run and leave us in control of the battlefield.

The Belt of Truth

What is the armor that the Christian is to wear? We find a description of it in Ephesians 6:14-17. The first piece of armor we are to put on is the girdle, or belt, of truth. In New Testament times, soldiers generally wore long, flowing robes, both in battle and in their other activities. During a battle, they would tuck their robes in the belt around their waist so their legs would be free for fighting and running. When a soldier dressed for battle, the belt was the last piece of armor to be put on. In addition to its purpose of girding up the loins, the belt also served to secure the rest of the armor. Just as the soldier's belt encircled his body and held his armor snugly in place, so truth binds the Christian's armor together and leaves him unencumbered for the battle.

What is the truth being described in this passage? The Word of God defines truth for us in several places. This truth is best seen in Jesus Christ, who is the personification of truth. In John 14:6 Jesus stated, "I am the way, the truth, and the life."

In John 17:17 we are given another definition of truth: "Sanctify them through thy truth: thy word is truth." Here we see that the Bible is truth. These two aspects of truth—the Living Word and the written Word—when brought together form the Christian's belt of truth.

We face an Enemy who is called the father of lies (see John 8:44). Satan is the embodiment of deceit. While he often appears as an angel of light, in reality he brings despair, darkness and death. Such an enemy can be overcome only by truth. And Christ is that truth. Thus, victory over Satan comes only through Christ. In His light we will see the Devil's deceptions for what they really are.

God's Word is our source for knowing the Truth. This is one reason why a daily devotional time in the Word is so vital. It enables us to know Christ more intimately and to discover His truth. It is important for us to get used to the feel of the armor and to have it properly adjusted before we enter the battle. We must come to know Christ in a very personal way if we want to be victorious in the fight.

This was Paul's desire when he cried, "That I may know him, and the power of his resurrection" (Phil. 3:10). What Paul was talking about here is more than head knowledge of the historical facts relating to Christ. While this type of knowledge is necessary, it is not sufficient in itself. We need to know that we are united to Christ in an indissoluble union.

Brass is a combination of zinc and copper. When these two elements are melted and fused together, they form the new metal. Once brass has been formed, it can never be broken down into the two base metals again. This is a beautiful picture of our union with Christ. We are so bonded to Him that we actually become one new person. Christ is the Head, and we are members of His Body. Nothing Satan can do, no matter how hard he tries, will separate us from the love of God that is in Christ Jesus our Lord (see Rom. 8:35-39).

It is important to note here that this passage is not endorsing the idea that such security allows people to sin and then find excuses for it. But neither do I find any room in the Word for teaching that belittles the finished work of Calvary and makes it ineffective. When we are born again, we are given a new life in Christ and are so joined to Him that nothing can separate us. He is our life; therefore, we begin to live the way He would live. Christ places His truth in us, and it becomes part of us.

Putting on the belt of truth is basic to our entire Christian experience. That is why God has given us this piece of armor first rather than last.

The Breastplate of Righteousness

The Christian's second piece of spiritual armor is the breastplate of righteousness (see Eph. 6:14). The breastplate worn by a Roman soldier covered both the front and back of his body, providing protection for the vital organs. In the same way, the breastplate of righteousness protects the spiritual heart of man—his emotions and desires.

This righteousness is found in Christ. It is His righteousness that enables the believer to stand before God uncondemned. If we fail in the Christian life, as we all do at times, our position before God in Christ does not change—even though Satan will try to convince us otherwise. Our position before God is not established on the basis of the good we have done or the obedience we have rendered. For this reason Satan's accusations, even though well grounded, cannot move us from God's presence. We stand there in Christ's righteousness—not our own.

Unfortunately, many Christians today have not seen this truth in the Word. This gives Satan an opportunity to cause discouragement and fear in their lives. Having failed to grasp the truth of their righteous standing in Christ, these believers fall ready victims to the Deceiver. Some of them even go so far as to doubt their salvation and to fear that they have committed the unpardonable sin.

On the other hand, Satan often uses the fact of our safety in Christ to persuade the Christian that he can live as he pleases since he is fully protected before God and Christ. This is the problem that the nation of Israel had in the Old Testament. When Balaam found that he could not destroy the Children of Israel because they stood secure in God's favor, he devised a strategy that led many of the Israelites to reject God's command concerning total separation and to marry outside their nation (see Num. 22:1—25:3). Balaam reasoned to himself that when the Israelites began to fraternize with the ungodly nations around them, then God would be forced to destroy His people. While God did find it necessary to chasten the Children of Israel and set them aside for a time, His judgment was only temporary.

So it is among Christians today. Many believers have refused to live an obedient life, and consequently, God has been forced to judge them temporarily, because their experiences of defeat were dishonoring to Him. They cannot be used again until they come to the place where they recognize their failure and see that their strength and forgiveness lies in Christ.

I have found one verse in the Bible that, while not normally considered to refer to this subject, is very effective in our battles with Satan. Matthew 5:25 states, "Agree with thine adversary quickly." Many times we can defeat an enemy quicker by agreeing with him rather than opposing him. When Satan comes and points his finger at me and says, "See what sin you committed again," I admit my wrong immediately. I agree with him quickly on that point; then I remind him that I am standing on Christ's righteousness and not my own. Because of this great truth, I can tell the Devil to leave. Then I fall on my knees and confess the matter to the Lord. We do not find victory by excusing our sins. If we confess them and forsake them by the grace of God, we will find that Christ works His righteousness in us in our everyday experience. Thus, the breastplate of righteousness becomes an effective part of our armor.

Having been declared righteous in Christ, we need to live a righteous life while on earth. The righteousness of Christ has been accounted to us; therefore, we are pronounced righteous before God. But to see only this side of salvation can be very harmful. Romans 6:18 tells us that we are servants of righteousness. Later in that same chapter we read: "But now being made free from sin, and become servants to God, ye have your fruit unto holiness, and the end everlasting life" (v. 22). Paul was saying that in order to be identified with Christ in His life, we must also be identified with Him in His death. When He died to sin, we died to sin, and because of that we have been set free from the power and bondage of sin. Just as the Israelites were set free from the bondage of Egypt when they were led out of the land, so we have been potentially set free from the bondage of sin by accepting Christ as Saviour. However, this truth must be applied in our daily lives, for only when we have truly died to sin is righteous living produced in us.

We find this teaching presented again in Galatians 5:16, where we read that the person who is truly walking by the Spirit will not fulfill the lusts of the flesh. God will apply what Jesus provided for us by His death—deliverance from sin. He will also apply what Jesus has provided for us by His life—the fruit of the Holy Spirit. The Holy Spirit will enable us to live a righteous life. The righteousness of Christ and the righteous life we can live in the Spirit is the breastplate that will protect our soul (mind, emotions and will) from Satan's arrows.

Shoes of the Gospel of Peace

The third piece of armor described in Ephesians 6 is the shoes of the Gospel of peace (see v. 15). This verse reminds me of the words of Isaiah, who said, "How beautiful upon the mountains are the feet of him that bringeth good tidings, that publisheth peace" (Isa. 52:7). In this passage the emphasis is on the witness who is giving the message of the Gospel. I personally believe that the Ephesians passage is stressing the Gospel message itself, the message of peace, rather than the one carrying it. The Gospel is not a message of confusion or of fear. It provides a peace that cancels out fear.

Once again, this particular piece of armor can have more than one application attached to it. First, the Gospel of peace refers to peace *with* God that is established through faith in Jesus Christ. Romans 5:1 describes this phase of peace: "Therefore being justified by faith, we have peace with God through our Lord Jesus Christ." The reference here is to our position before the Lord. As Christians, our position before God never changes; thus, we will enjoy peace with Him for eternity.

Satan cannot do anything to disturb our peace with God. Our foundation stands sure. Though the Devil may throw his fiery darts at us, we can stand against him and tell him that the peace he is seeking to disturb is not ours—and not his—but God's. No power in heaven or on earth can touch that peace.

The second application of the Gospel of peace refers to our daily experience as believers. This peace *of* God is spoken of in Philippians 4:7: "The peace of God, which passeth all understanding." In our daily walk with Christ, we enjoy this peace as we follow the conditions laid down in His Word.

The conditions we are to follow are also stated in this passage: "Be careful for nothing [don't be anxious]; but in every thing by prayer and supplication with thanksgiving let your requests be made known unto God. And the peace of God, which passeth all understanding, shall keep your hearts and minds through Christ Jesus" (vv. 6,7). When we give our problems to God through prayer and thank Him for His care for us, then we will be filled with the peace of God. This is the peace of which Jesus spoke when He said, "Peace I leave with you, my peace I give unto you: not as the world giveth, give I unto you. Let not your heart be troubled, neither let it be afraid" (John 14:27).

What a glorious promise! Christ has left us His peace. He died to make it ours, and through the Holy Spirit, He maintains it in our hearts. He not only *left* it for us—He *gave* it to us. He not only died, leaving us an inheritance, but He also rose from the grave to be the executor of His own will.

Not only should we possess this peace as part of our own armor, but we should also be ready to impart it to others. The Twentieth Century New Testament translates Ephesians 6:15: "With the readiness to serve the Good News of Peace as shoes for your feet." Regardless of how bad the circumstances may appear to be, we should go forth and proclaim the Gospel of the peace of God. It is this deep-seated peace, found only in Him, that enables us to endure the fierce battles against evil.

The Shield of Faith

The Christian's next piece of equipment is the shield of faith. With this shield we are able to quench all the fiery darts of the Wicked One (see Eph. 6:16). The Roman shield was large and, when properly used, protected the soldier's entire body from the arrows of the enemy. The shield would not only stop an arrow but would also deflect a sword thrust. But, in order to be useful, the soldier had to have his shield with him at all times during battle.

In Romans 10:17 we are told that "faith cometh by hearing, and hearing by the word of God." Thus, we possess the shield of faith when the Word of God is firmly implanted not only in our minds but also in our hearts. We need to memorize the Word, believe it and obey it so that we can cling to its truths and its promises when Satan throws his darts at us. He cannot touch us when we skillfully use our shield. The psalmist said, "Thy word have I hid in mine heart, that I might not sin against thee" (Ps. 119:11). Earlier in the same chapter we read: "Wherewithal shall a young man cleanse his way? by taking heed thereto according to thy word" (v. 9).

A good illustration of a person who wore the shield of faith is Abraham. God promised him that he would be the father of many nations. The Bible later records Abraham's response to God's promise: "And being not weak in faith, he considered not his own body now dead, when he was about an hundred years old, neither yet the deadness of Sarah's womb: he staggered not at the promise of God through unbelief; but was strong in faith, giving glory to God; and being fully persuaded that, what he had promised, he was able to perform" (Rom. 4:19-21). It is no wonder that Abraham is called the "father of faith." He simply believed that what God had promised, He was able to fulfill.

Job is another example of a man who wore his armor victoriously. Satan accused God of putting a hedge around Job. He was right, for God was protecting His servant—something He does for all of His children.

Satan asked God to allow him to afflict Job, believing that in the face of such affliction Job would curse God. Permission was granted, but God set limits for Satan regarding how far he could go in testing Job. The Devil destroyed Job's possessions and his family and even inflicted this already suffering man with painful boils. But regardless of what Satan did, Job did not sin. He was a man who stood the test. Even when his wife urged him to curse God and die, Job would not listen. He said God had sent him into this world without anything, and if He wanted him to leave it without anything, that was His right. Job did not lose his faith because his goods and his family were gone; he stood on the solid foundation provided by God and found that the Lord's armor protected him. Job was not a perfect man, but he was victorious in his testings. He made good use of the shield of faith in his conflict.

When we are being tested, we must always remember that God is sovereign. He will not allow us to be tested beyond what we are able to endure but will give us a way of escape from each testing (see I Cor. 10:13). If you have the shield of faith that comes from relying on the Word of God, then you will emerge from your testings like gold that has been refined and purified by fire (see I Pet. 1:7).

One of the special darts that Satan uses against Christians is that of causing them to doubt their salvation. If the shield of faith is wielded correctly at the proper time, it will protect us from this dart. Some of God's people, as we have noted before, go so far as to believe they have committed the unpardonable sin when this doubt strikes. The solution to this doubt is to rely on Christ's promise in God's Word that "He that heareth my word, and believeth on him that sent me, hath everlasting life, and shall not come into condemnation; but is passed from death unto life" (John 5:24). Use that great promise against the Enemy. He cannot face it.

The story is told of a boy who was saved in a mission. He knew very little about the Gospel, but when it was presented to him, he accepted Christ as his Saviour. He was given a New Testament, and the promise in John 5:24 was impressed on his heart and mind. That night when he went to bed, the Devil began to work on his mind, saying, "So you think you have religion?" The little boy hardly knew what to say, but he argued back with these words: "The preacher said I have it, the Bible says I have it, even though you, Satan, say I don't." Finally, the boy opened up his New Testament to John 5:24 and, with his finger on the passage, shoved the Bible under the bed and said, "Devil, see for yourself." The Tempter left him. Satan could not penetrate that shield of faith.

The Helmet of Salvation

Another vital part of the Christian's armor is the helmet of salvation (see Eph. 6:17). The helmet was one of the most important pieces of a soldier's armor because it protected his head from injury. The helmet was also the only part of the armor that gave complete protection to the wearer. While the belt and the breastplate only covered part of the area they were intended to protect, the helmet completely encircled the head, protecting it from attack no matter which way the head was turned. Unlike the shield, which only guarded the person when he was using it properly, the helmet was continually shielding the head from the enemy's weapons.

In order for the rest of the armor to be effective, a person must first put on the helmet of Christ's salvation. Jesus Christ Himself is that salvation (see Ps. 27:1). Having accepted Him as Saviour, we receive forgiveness for our sins and eternal life with Him (see I John 5:11,12). Like a helmet, Christ's salvation completely covers us and protects us. Once we have received His salvation, it will not be removed (see John 10:28,29). We will be victorious in our fight with Satan if we realize that salvation is not just something that the Lord gives to us—salvation is Christ Himself living in us.

The head is the control center of the body. When we accept Christ, He seeks to guide our thoughts and plans, enabling us to have the peace of God. But often we ignore the Lord's leading. Then when our minds are in a state of turmoil due to difficulties and strife, Satan uses the occasion to throw his darts at us. Sometimes he gets in his most effective blows when the body is weakened by illness, lack of food or some severe strain.

A missionary to China for many years was captured and placed in a concentration camp. She was finally freed and allowed to return home. She arrived in this country victorious and rejoicing. However, her body had been greatly weakened by the harsh and cruel treatment she had received in the camp. Thus, shortly after her return, Satan penetrated her armor with one of his fiery darts. He did so by misusing the verse "If any man be in Christ, he is a new creature: old things are passed away; behold, all things are become new" (II Cor. 5:17). Satan was able to cause her to interpret this verse out of its context and to appraise falsely her own conduct and desires. She soon began to wonder if she was really saved.

She wrote to me for help. I wrote back and told her what the verse meant. The meaning of this passage was completely different from what the Devil had interpreted it to mean to her. Satan had convinced this woman that this passage was telling her that all her old habits and sinful attitudes should have left her immediately when she accepted Christ and that she should never have had the tendency to sin again. However, this verse is really saying to us that when we accept Christ, a new spiritual life is born in us so that we can have communion with God. When the Lord Jesus was on the earth, the disciples had fellowship with Him face to face. But after He went back to glory, they still had fellowship with Him, though on a different basis. All things became new for them. Their fellowship with Him was in the Spirit and not in the flesh. This is true of us also.

The missionary wrote back and thanked me for the help I gave her. Her problems had been created because she had temporarily laid aside her helmet of salvation; therefore, Satan had taken advantage of her.

Because of Christ's salvation and presence in us, we can call on Him to protect our mind and heart from Satan's attempts to control them. Hebrews 7:25 promises us, "He is able also to save them to the uttermost that come unto God by him, seeing he ever liveth to make intercession for them." When the Devil seeks to wound our conscience with some sin we have committed, we need to remember that Jesus Christ, our Advocate, cleanses us from all sin when we confess it to Him (see I John 1:7,9).

In addition to the salvation Christ gives to us, the wearing of the helmet of salvation also carries with it the idea of preparing our mind for battle. We must learn to discipline our thoughts so we can protect our mind against the imaginations of evil that plague us, both from without and from within. By wearing the helmet of salvation properly, we will learn how to bring every thought into captivity to Christ (see II Cor. 10:5). Mental control is one of our greatest needs today, and we will find it adequately supplied through the helmet Christ provides.

The Sword of the Spirit

To complete our armor we are told to take the sword of the Spirit, which is the Word of God (see Eph. 6:17). God's Word is our weapon against Satan's attacks. Like any weapon, we must always be prepared to use this sword at a moment's notice. Satan will not wait until we have our Bibles open and are reading them before he attacks us. He strikes at the times when our minds may be far from the Word. This danger can be met, however, if we have memorized a number of passages. The Spirit of the Lord will bring these verses to our attention as the need arises. When the Word of God becomes a vital and integral part of our lives, then we will be well equipped to ward off Satan's attacks.

For this reason, we should be serious in our efforts to memorize the Word of God. While it is true that children and young people can memorize easier than those who are older, age does not need to be a barrier to memory work. Older adults will simply have to work harder in order to retain the passages they are seeking to memorize.

Our Saviour's testing in the wilderness is a graphic illustration of the power of God's Word in overcoming Satan's attacks (see Matt. 4:1-11). Regardless of what kind of temptation the Devil used in testing the Lord, Christ's response always began with the words "It is written." In the face of temptation, Jesus defended Himself by using the Word of God. Satan simply could not fight Christ's arguments because they were based on the Word.

The expression "It is written" could also be translated, "It has been written, and it stands written today." The Word of God is just as true now as it was the first time it was spoken. When properly used, Satan cannot stand against the Scriptures today any more than he could when our Saviour used them so effectively almost 2000 years ago.

Satan is not beyond using the Word of God himself. He often quotes only part of a passage, uses the verses out of context or changes the meaning of the passage entirely in order to deceive us and lead us astray. I believe it can be safely said that a close examination of any passage Satan has twisted to deceive us also contains the correction for that false teaching.

The degree to which we will be able to use the sword of the Spirit will depend on the degree to which we allow it to penetrate our hearts. The Word of God is sharper than a two-edged sword (see Heb. 4:12). It not only reveals what is in a person's heart, but it will also help us to discern between God's truth and Satan's lies. However, in order to be effective, it must first pierce our hearts before it can be used as a powerful weapon in leading souls to Christ or in defeating Satan when he opposes us.

The Resource of Prayer

As the Christian puts on the armor of God and enters the battle against Satan, he has one additional resource that will sustain him in the fight—prayer. Ephesians 6:18 tells us, "Praying always with all prayer and supplication in the Spirit, and watching thereunto with all perseverance and supplication for all saints."

The expression "praying always" suggests the importance of remaining alert and of praying at all times and under all conditions. This passage also instructs us to employ various kinds of prayer in our struggle with Satan. Prayer is not limited to our quiet times alone. We can pray in public as well as in private, can utter both long prayers and short prayers—whatever kind of prayer is needed. We can pray anytime and anywhere—audibly and inaudibly—as long as our prayers are in the Spirit.

In addition, the words "all prayer" would suggest that our prayers should have all the elements of prayer in them. They should include more than asking for and receiving something. Praise, thanksgiving, confession, petition and supplication should also be included. Our prayers should also be specific, naming particular people and their individual needs, as well as our own specific requests. One reason so many Christians have ineffective prayer lives is because their prayers are often vague.

Not only does prayer aid the believer in his spiritual warfare, but prayer itself is also a battle. Daniel realized this when his prayer was hindered (see Dan. 10:12,13). Our Saviour, we are told, was in agony when He prayed in Gethsemane (see Luke 22:44). The word "agony" can also be translated "conflict" or "fight." In Ephesians 6 prayer is once again linked with the believer's conflict. However, while prayer is a battle, it is a fight we will win when we persevere, for Satan is no match for our prayers any more than he is for God's Word.

Someone has said, "Prayer is not trying to persuade God to join us in our service for Him. It is joining Him in His service. Prayer is a true Christian laying hold by faith on property which Satan controls, but which rightly belongs to God; and holding on until Satan lets go."

Ephesians 6:18 also exhorts us to pray for all the saints. Our fellow believers are involved in the same spiritual battle we are and need the support that prayer can give them. Only God knows how many believers have fallen by the wayside because of lack of prayer support. At a time when satanic forces are achieving great success in dividing God's people, it is vital that believers everywhere enter into a spiritual union and contend for each other's spiritual well-being through prayer. When we join together and fight side by side against Satan's forces with the Lord's help, we will be victorious.

The Gospel is not popular today. Courage is needed to proclaim it. We need to pray for each other as Paul prayed, "That I may open my mouth boldly, to make known the mystery of the gospel"

(v. 19). God forbid that we should sin against each other by failing to pray for one another.

We are fighting a defeated foe. Christ won victory over Satan for us at the cross. While the Devil is still free to roam the earth for the present and has some power granted to him by God, his victories are only temporary. However, Satan's forces are powerless against us when we use the armor God has given us for the conflict.

Chapter 7

Why Is Satan Still at Large?

Satan's presence or absence in the world makes a tremendous difference in the actions of people. At the present Satan has access to heaven as well as to earth. Even though the Devil's powers have been limited by God and though he does not continually roam the earth, evil continues to increase in the world. Man is committing every kind of lewd and violent act imaginable.

The time will come, however, when Satan will be chained for 1000 years and the earth will experience a period of righteousness and peace that has not existed since the fall of man. Following the thousand years, Satan will be loosed for a little season and will be allowed to have free rein on the earth. During that time a great host of men and women, who yielded only feigned allegiance to God through the 1000-year period, will follow the Archdeceiver. As a result, they will be judged by fire at the battle of Gog and Magog.

As we have seen in earlier chapters, Satan has been defeated by Christ. He has already been judged and sentenced to eternity in hell, the place prepared especially for him and his angels. However, God has allowed him to have some power and influence over man in this age. As a result of Satan's influence, many people are being led down the path of sin. Why, then, does God allow Satan to remain active and loose at the present time? To this question we can submit only a partial answer.

The enemies of God have claimed victory in the spiritual battle for the world. While this may appear to be true today, eventually the record will disclose the full evidence of Satan's colossal failures, in spite of all his boasts and ambitions. When the record is completed, the whole evil world, including the forces of Satan, will be silenced. Multitudes of people will be convinced of their guilt as sinners.

Many people today have brushed aside the Lord's warnings about His future judgment and punishment of those who have ignored His Word. However, the day is coming when this will no longer be possible. The record will be inescapable. In the light of God's truth and righteousness, these people will stand self-condemned before Him. Even now, God has passed judgment on unregenerate man, but that judgment has not yet been executed. His grace has withheld the day of wrath, but God will not restrain His anger forever.

The constant presence of evil in the world means that the Christian is faced with a continual war against sin and Satan. God has allowed this war to continue for a specific purpose. Only by entering into this warfare can the Christian learn how to be an overcomer through the power of Christ. This causes the believer's character to be developed in a way that would not be possible otherwise.

Moreover, the Lord has left His followers on the earth to be His witnesses (see Acts 1:8,9). Often the Christian must witness in the midst of great opposition. But as he witnesses and as he serves the Lord in other capacities, he lays up treasures in heaven for himself. Our serving in the midst of trials on earth delights the heart of God and leads to greater crowns of glory in heaven.

The fact that God often uses Satan in His process of developing the character of the Christian can be seen in the life of Job. Satan sought and gained God's permission to test Job. While Satan's purpose for this testing was to cause Job to reject God, the Lord used it to strengthen his faith even more. The same is true in our lives as well. Satan brings testings against the child of God in order to cause him to fail. God, on the other hand, allows such testings so that the believer might grow stronger and become more Christlike. Though Satan intends such testings for evil, God works them together for good (see Rom. 8:28).

The life of Peter also illustrates this truth. In Luke 22:31, the Lord warned Peter that Satan desired to take control of him and to sift him like wheat. But Jesus went on to assure His disciple that He was praying for him. The Lord added that when Peter had passed the test, he would be of even greater service to God, for he would then be able to strengthen his fellow believers. Peter's faith did falter for a time. He tried to kill a man in the Garden of

Gethsemane, he denied knowing the Lord three times, and he forgot Christ's promise to rise again from the dead. But in the Book of the Acts, we see Peter rise above these testings to become a powerful witness for the Lord and a leader in the early church.

There is nothing in this universe, whether a power or a personality, that is not subject to God. He is sovereign in His universe. Though we may not be able to give a reason for everything that happens to us, we know that, just as the universe was designed by God to fit His plan, our lives have been planned by Him. He controls our destiny when we submit fully to His leadership.

Part of God's plan for us includes being tested by the Enemy. Satan's attacks are used by God to develop Christlike character in us. When we persevere in these battles, we receive eternal rewards. The Lord intends for us to be victorious in our spiritual warfare with Satan. He has already won the war for us. In addition, He has given us the armor and weapons we need for the day-to-day battles. Therefore, we should not fear our fight with Satan but should instead welcome the opportunities to strengthen our faith. We have the Lord on our side, and we can win the war against Satan when we boldly face the Enemy in the power of Christ.

Back to the Bible is a nonprofit ministry dedicated to Bible teaching, evangelism and edification of Christians worldwide.

If we may assist you in knowing more about Christ and the Christian life, please write to us without obligation:

Back to the Bible
P.O. Box 82808
Lincoln, NE 68501